Knowlton School of Architecture,
The Ohio State University

SOURCE BOOKS
IN ARCHITECTURE

3

BERNARD TSCHUMI

Zénith de Rouen
Rouen, France

Todd Gannon and Laurie A. Gunzelman, Volume Editors

Series Editors
Todd Gannon and Jeffrey Kipnis

Princeton Architectural Press, New York

Published by
Princeton Architectural Press
37 East Seventh Street
New York, New York 10003

For a free catalog of books, call 1.800.722.6657.
Visit our Web site at www.papress.com.

Editor: Jennifer N. Thompson
Designers: Lorraine Wild and Robert Ruehlman

Special thanks to: Nettie Aljian, Ann Alter, Nicola
Bednarek, Janet Behning, Megan Carey, Penny Chu,
Russell Fernandez, Jan Haux, Clare Jacobson, Mark
Lamster, Nancy Eklund Later, Linda Lee, Nancy
Levinson, Katharine Myers, Jane Sheinman, Scott
Tennent, and Deb Wood of Princeton Architectural Press
—Kevin C. Lippert, publisher

Library of Congress Cataloging-in-Publication Data
Tschumi, Bernard, 1944-
  Bernard Tschumi, Zénith de Rouen / Todd Gannon and
Laurie A.
Gunzelman, volume editors.
    p. cm. -- (Source books in architecture ; 3)
  ISBN 1-56898-382-4 (pbk. : alk. paper)
  1. Zénith (Rouen, France) 2. Tschumi, Bernard, 1944-
3. Rouen
(France)--Buildings, structures, etc. I. Gannon, Todd.
II. Gunzleman,
Laurie A. III. Title. IV. Series.
  NA4178.R68 Z468 2003
  720'.92--dc21
                                        2003000330

Following the example of music publication, Source Books in Architecture offers an alternative to the traditional architectural monograph. If one is interested in hearing music, he or she simply purchases the desired recording. If, however, one wishes to study a particular piece in greater depth, it is possible to purchase the score—the written code that more clearly elucidates the structure, organization, and creative process that brings the work into being. This series is offered in the same spirit. Each Source Book focuses on a single work by a particular architect or on a special topic in contemporary architechture. The work is documented with sketches, models, renderings, working drawings, and photographs at a level of detail that allows complete and careful study of the project from its conception to the completion of design and construction.

The graphic component is accompanied by commentary from the architect and critics that further explores both the technical and cultural content of the work in question.

Source Books in Architecture was conceived by Jeffrey Kipnis and is the product of the Herbert Baumer seminars, a series of interactions between students and seminal practitioners at the Knowlton School of Architecture at The Ohio State University. Based on a significant amount of research on distinguished architects, students lead a discussion that encourages the architects to reveal their architectural motivations and techniques. The students then record and transcribe the meetings, which become the basis of these Source Books.

The seminars are made possible by a generous bequest of Herbert Herndon Baumer. Educated at the Ecole des Beaux-Arts, Baumer was a professor in the Department of Architecture at The Ohio State University from 1922 to 1956. He had a dual career as a distinguished design professor who inspired many students and a noted architect who designed several buildings at The Ohio State University and other Ohio colleges.

ACKNOWLEDGMENTS

This book would not have been possible without Bernard Tschumi and the staff at Bernard Tschumi Architects, in particular Véronique Descharrières and Alex Reid, as well as Hugh Dutton Associates, who provided a fabulous subject. Liz Kim, Lizzie Hodges, and Sylviane Brossard assisted with access to images, drawings, and the building itself.

Robert Livesey, director of the Knowlton School of Architecture, has provided continual encouragement and support. The input and advice of friends and colleagues, especially George Acock, Mike Cadwell, Tracy Gannon, Jackie Gargus, Carolyn Hank, and José Oubrerie, have been essential.

Thanks are due to the participants in the 1997 Baumer seminars: Matt Bernhardt, Shane Chandler, Shawn Conyers, Kostandinos Fakelis, Marty Fenlon, Tony Freitag, Dan Haar, Patricia George, John Hardt, Sara Lahman, Scott Lesicko, Woo-Jin Lim, Kamal Mohey, Aimee Moore, Paul Mudry, Javier Págan, Ryan Palider, Susan Plaisted, Doug Scholl, Chris Shrodes, David Tyler, Michael Wetmore, and especially to Joe Moss, who compiled the initial research.

Kevin Lippert and Jennifer Thompson of Princeton Architectural Press and graphic designers Lorraine Wild and Robert Ruehlman provided thoughtful production and design. Considerable contributions were also made by Bhakti Bania, Bharat Baste, Mike Denison, Rujuta Mody, and Manoj Patel. Acock Associates Architects and Atlas Blueprint and Supply both generously supported the project, and Vi Schaaf cheerfully kept the finances in order.

Finally, special thanks go to Jeffrey Kipnis, for his continued mentoring and collaboration, and to Nicole Hill, for her unbelievable patience.

March 1998	July 1998	November 1998	February 1999
Competition	Schematic Design	Design Development	Construction Documents

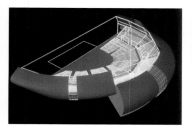

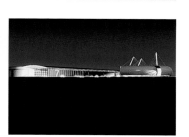

December 1999	14 February 2001	23 February 2001
Start of Construction	Project Completion	Public Opening

January 2001

September 2000

May 2000

Zénith de Rouen
Rouen, France

Owner:
District of Rouen

Location:
Rouen, France

Seating Capacity:
7,000

Exhibition Square Footage:
70,000

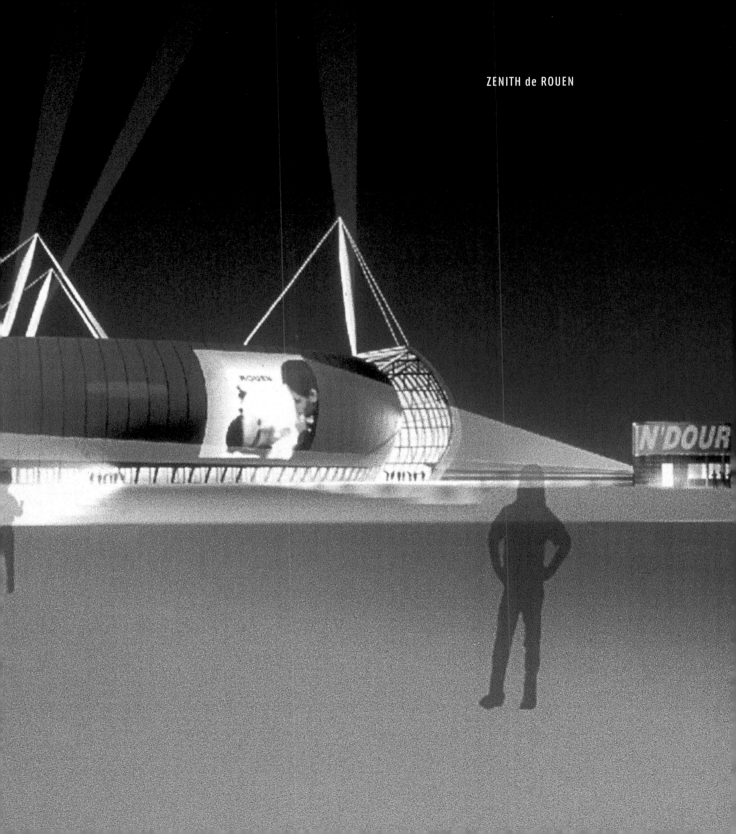

ZENITH de ROUEN

CONVERSATIONS WITH BERNARD TSCHUMI

Compiled and Edited by Todd Gannon

The following has been extracted from a series of exchanges between Bernard Tschumi and the students and faculty of the Knowlton School of Architecture that took place between 1999 and 2002.

Bernard Tschumi: While finishing my studies at the Federal Institute of Technology (ETH) in Zurich, I went to work for a year in Paris at the firm of Candilis-Josic-Woods. Within a few months, all hell broke loose. The events of May 1968 were felt around the world and with particular intensity in France. Nothing was the same after that. For some architects, it meant that they could no longer practice the corporate tenets of the modern movement.

In the early seventies, architecture formed two camps. On the one hand, we had a group, represented in the United States by Robert Venturi and in Europe by Aldo Rossi, who attempted to erase political tensions with a desire to make things friendly and palatable through historical allusions and analogies. On the other hand, we had radicals such as Superstudio, Archizoom, and Cedric Price pursuing projects with strong political and critical goals but with few intentions of ever building anything. For the built environment itself, this left little hope.

My own reaction was a decision to build nothing until I knew what I was doing. The following year I went to teach at the Architectural Association in London. Here, in the company of incredible artists with a conceptual

outlook—Richard Hamilton, Meret Oppenheim, the Beckers and others—I nurtured an obsession: I was determined to exploit the city for political and cultural purposes. For me, the city became a place of invention, a place of discovery, a place of appropriation. The events of '68 impressed upon me a deep suspicion of the ability of architecture, of any object, to effect social change. Architecture could only be political in relation to events.

This thinking provoked in me a fascination with the powers of conflict, of violence. Yet I soon realized an undeniable power in the opposite, in pleasure. Could there be a parallel in architecture to the physical pleasures of the skin? Did architecture harbor erotic potential?

Jeffrey Kipnis: Sex, violence, and excess constitute major conceptual themes throughout your body of work. But before we get to the specific agenda of the projects, I want to explore the general possibilities of excess in architecture through the writings of Georges Bataille, whose thought, I believe, parallels the development of your early work.

In addition to writing about the impossibility of architecture, Bataille posited that the question of authenticity in contemporary life was located in the problem of excess. As traditional architecture is obliged to serve existing power structures, it is also obliged to suppress the possibilities of excess and spontaneity. Does this relate to your refusal to participate in traditional practice?

View of entry hall,
Rouen Concert Hall,
Rouen, France, 1998–2001

BT: Perhaps. You do not get a job in architecture unless you get along with power . . .

Bataille's thinking has certainly influenced my own. His work has been analyzed in an interesting book by Denis Hollier called *Against Architecture.* Here he makes the distinction, which I have elaborated upon in my own writings, between the pyramid and the labyrinth, between concept and experience. He then develops an extraordinary discourse dealing with life and death and more importantly, the moment of passage from one state to the other. I argue that this limit, the place where you cross the boundary, is erotic.

Of course, other writings demand our attention as well. The history of ideas in the last quarter of a century has to deal with the work of Foucault, Barthes, Deleuze, Derrida, and so on. Their ideas constitute a way of looking at the world.

JK: It is important for us to discuss these writings, but I do not want to give the impression that the philosophy somehow takes precedence over the work itself or even over the techniques that produce it. My goal here is to investigate how an architect gathers the materials necessary to develop an independent architectural personality.

In the *Manhattan Transcripts,* for instance, you were investigating a number of issues: the *dérive,* ideas of circulation and urbanism, even the Situationists' map of Paris. Can you comment upon the influence of these items on the development of the *Transcripts*?

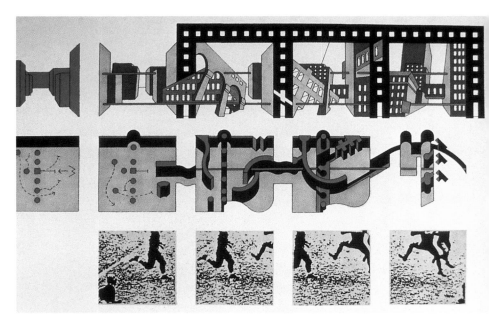

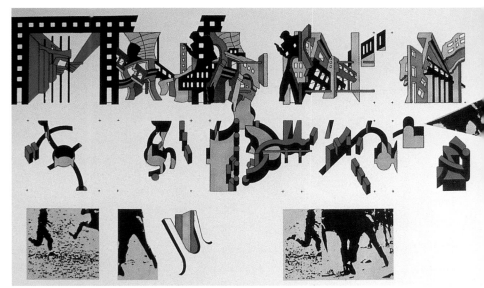

Excerpt from the *Manhattan Transcripts,* 1976–81

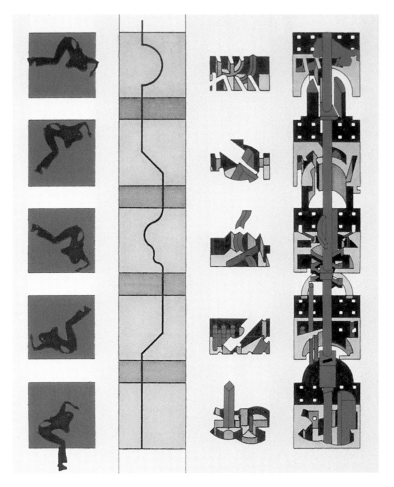

Excerpt from the *Manhattan Transcripts*, 1976–81

BT: Quite often architects borrow models from other disciplines to help clarify and understand what they are doing. That general context of ideas is important; it represents the culture of the time. In the eighteenth century, Durand borrowed from radical advances in biology and the natural sciences to develop his theory of typology in architecture. Today it is no different.

It is in this sense that I consider the Situationists to be important. In response to their work, I became fascinated with the idea that one could map out a performance in an instrumentalized fashion. This research led me to study the phenomenon of notation in many disciplines: music, dance, even sports . . .

I arrived in New York in 1976. There, after a seven-year hiatus, I began to draw again. It was necessary because, although I had developed a focused critical attitude, I lacked a mode of visual expression. These early explorations in drawing, which culminated in the *Manhattan Transcripts,* mark a deliberate search for a way of working.

At the time, architects like Raimund Abraham were developing stunning drawings that were much better than any concurrent built work. I became fascinated with the possibilities of unbuilt architecture. Perhaps the real culture of architecture occurred on paper. Here one was free to introduce elements of pop culture, politics, film. Freed from the constraints of building, architectural research became a venue for provocative projects that did not necessarily have to be built to be considered real.

Thus I began my own investigations in architectural drawing. During the four years it took to complete the *Transcripts,* I also undertook other exercises that could be completed quickly, usually in the course of one night. I called them the *Screenplays*.

The idea was simple: I would take up a theme and see just how far I could push it. Often these themes came from film. I was intrigued by the technique of montage, which had to do with the rearrangement of reality through the sequential techniques of superimposition, as opposed to the contrived juxtapositions I observed in painting.

JK: There has always been a direct momentum toward technique in your work. You have said that after you drew the *Transcripts,* you realized that whatever their value as theoretical research, they gave you no clue on how to build. I am not sure that I agree with this assessment. While it is true that the *Transcripts* do not exhibit tectonic or material specificity, they are, by employing the instrumentality of hard-lined ink drawings, unequivocally about technique.

I think of other drawings that were contemporaneous with yours: Daniel Libeskind's highly personal *Chamber Works*, Peter Eisenman's hyper-analytical transformational studies, the collage strategies of Rem Koolhaas's *Exodus*. Of all these works, I would argue, yours are most closely tied to the legacy of architectural technique. Would you agree?

BT: I would like to think of the *Transcripts* as explorations in the construction of three-dimensional spaces. Indeed, these architects all explore the possibilities of architectural drawing in unique ways. My own explorations begin with variations on typical projection techniques—axonometrics, perspectives, and so on. Through a series of manipulations they become perverted and open the door to new possibilities.

In the case of the *Transcripts,* there are always three components: space, event, and movement. These simple components became, for me, a dynamic framework within which to explore the possibilities of architecture.

What these components lack, however, is a material component. Even though I was exploring architecture in terms of concepts, I ultimately wanted to tend toward built things. The crucial step, then, becomes the materialization of the concept. This, for me, became a definition of architecture.

JK: Rem, Peter, and Danny had to spend years to figure out how to turn their conceptualizations into technique. What is striking about your work is that the first conceptual moment is simultaneously proto-architectural.

BT: When I finished my studies, I felt that I had found a form of thinking to apply to any exercise or problem. I could write a play as an architect, I could make a movie as an architect, I could write philosophy as an architect. I would turn what you just said 180 degrees and say that my thinking is architectural before it is conceptual. I do not write in a linear fashion; I write spatially. For me, building and writing are very similar acts—both are methods of organizing thoughts in time and space.

JK: Our discussion has focused upon a period in which architecture was being rethought in terms of post structuralist linguistics. For architects, the typical course of action for taking up these problems was to abandon the question of space. Space was too loaded with a Hegelian metaphysical history, too close to an institutional ambition. As such, the discussion of space virtually disappeared from the discipline for almost ten years.

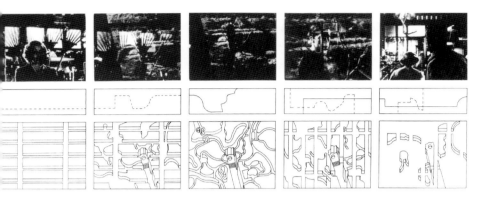

Excerpt from *Screenplays:* Alfred Hitchcock's *Psycho*

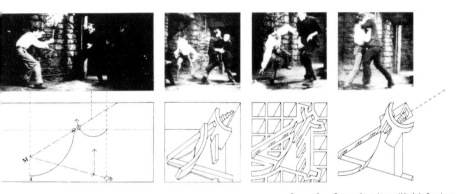

Excerpt from *Screenplays:* James Whale's *Frankenstein*

You were different. Not only did you refuse to give up the problem of space, you actually foregrounded it. Why do you cling so tightly to the notion of space?

BT: For the same reason that a fish would not question water. I believe certain components to be irreducible from architecture: space, event, and movement. My ambition, even in the theoretical work, has always been architecture. To remove the question of space eliminates the possibility of architecture.

JK: To take up the problem of space in architecture requires an acute sense of what constitutes and what constructs architectural space. Do you consciously work to develop this acuity? If so, what are the mechanisms you employ?

BT: Of course! It is crucial to develop this sense. Perhaps the best method is to visit the great buildings in history and analyze their spatial configurations and variations. Clearly this is not always possible, so one must also hone an ability to analyze drawings and photographs.

After you have done this for some time, you may begin to speculate that there are only so many moves to be made, that all the possible configurations of walls, floors, and ceilings have been exhausted. This thinking leads to the suspicious realm of typology. Typology relies on reduction: subtle differences are ignored in order to reinforce overt similarities. I would advise all of you to be on guard against this tendency. For in those differences that typology erases, those subtle contingencies of materiality and light, of movement and space, we might uncover entirely new possibilities for architecture—possibilities that refuse to conform to established typologies.

JK: Moments of self-reflection punctuate the life of any architect. The first occur early, when one searches for his issues, for a way to relate his own work to current thinking. They ask themselves, Should I change? What should I do next? How should I proceed? This process is crucial in order to develop a critical stance. Through it one gains the ability to think and speak intelligently about not only his or her own work, but also about the work of others.

After years of practice, an architect's thinking begins to change; he or she no longer needs to define himself or herself in terms of the vicissitudes of the discipline. At this stage, self-critical reflections become markedly different from youthful meditations. One might begin to wonder, How do I mature as an architect? What does it mean to begin the process of maturation?

BT: Let's not use the word *maturity*. I don't ever want to mature. I think what you want to know is whether an architect should aspire toward a certain coherence or totality that might be identifiable as a body of work. This is a very interesting question, one that plays a large part in what one will do next.

I'll recount two examples from my own experience. The first occurred about twenty years ago—a very happy time in my life. I had just finished the *Transcripts* and was beginning to enjoy a bit of a reputation. My enemies did not yet know me, and my friends were very supportive. I decided then to enter the competition for Le Parc de la Villette. After the work was under way, I became very disturbed, because I realized that I was breaking the continuity of what had been several years

Advertisements for Architecture, 1978

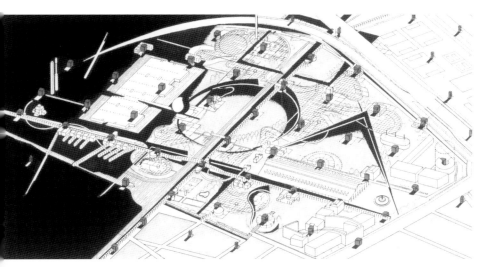

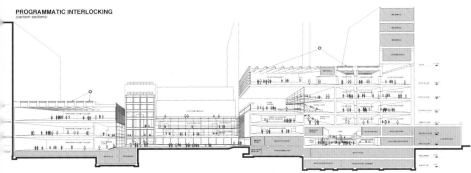

PROGRAMMATIC INTERLOCKING
(cartoon sections)

SECTION EE A section through the whole museum, showing the clear distribution of Temporary Exhibition galleries, Departmental galleries and Permanent Collection, all around the Sculpture Garden: the Sculpture Court, and the Sculpture Terrace. The interlocking between the old and the new (here cantilever) generates a new Upper Garden.

top: Axonmometric, Parc de la Villette,
Paris, France, 1982–98.

bottom: Section Perspective, MoMA Extension,
New York City, 1997

of successful research. All of a sudden I found myself dealing with the pressures of budgets, clients, construction, issues I had been specifically avoiding for years. Yet somehow I also felt an unbelievable excitement. These new influences propelled my work in totally new directions.

The second was the very strange summer in the late nineties I spent working on the MoMA competition. We had developed a strong scheme, and I believed that we had a very good chance of winning. You will not believe it, but this deeply worried me. I feared that winning the competition would turn me into a two-project architect. MoMA would have consumed the rest of my life. Was I really willing to define myself entirely in terms of La Villette and MoMA? If so, what sort of totality would that produce?

I guess I will never know, because someone else was selected for the MoMA extension. But the question remains, How does one define a body of work? Do you work toward a signature style? I think not.

JK: A signature style brings with it real dangers. If the exploration does not continue to deepen, one risks a kind of formulaic redundancy that might even be termed *self-plagiarism.*

BT: That's right. I would hate to be referred to as a signature architect. I would prefer "statement architect." I am much more interested in pursuing the research. I would be content to build just a few projects in my life, perhaps ten. But I want each one to result in a key statement about a particular architectural condition.

Todd Gannon: Do you ever set a level or single out a project that you have to compete with?

BT: Occasionally. In competitions this often happens. At La Villette, for example, I was competing against Krier's proposal, completed a few years earlier, for the same site. Competitions generate strange issues; they are often about ego and power. At the moment I am more interested in influence than power.

TG: Do you use other projects to stimulate your own ideas?

BT: Regardless of the politics involved, I am determined to set the issues of the project. I am not interested in pursuing overt relationships to past buildings. I leave that work to the critics.

Often the constraints themselves provide the energy to produce an original scheme. Le Fresnoy would be an example. I feel that one of our greatest strengths as an office is our ability to distill a complex program into a clear concept.

JK: Questions like these often arise in this sort of conversation. When John Lennon completed the *Imagine* album, for instance, he was asked in a television interview what music he was listening to. He replied that he used to listen to a lot of music, but now he only likes to write it. This marks a profound transition: he ceases to be audience/producer and becomes solely producer. From that point on, the musical problems he solves are not derived in terms of other work, but rather internally.

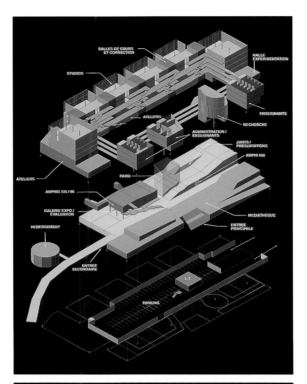

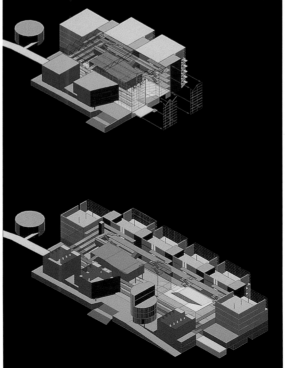

School of Architecture,
Marne-la-Vallée, France, 1996

BT: Orson Welles used to say, "I don't like cinema. I like making cinema."

JK: Exactly. At a certain stage, one's body of work should become sufficiently rich that it will generate its own line of investigation. One may not know where the next project will come from, but he will know where he/she wants to go architecturally.

BT: Yes but I worry that you make things sound simpler than they actually are. I admit that I maintain a nebulous area of interests I wish to explore, but for me the direction is not so focused. Some ideas may have been partially investigated; others may constitute new avenues of exploration. I take advantage of the possibility of each commission to exploit one or several of these avenues. If I am lucky, I might discover new ones along the way.

JK: Does this mean that you reflect back upon your own work and decide which investigations have been fully resolved and which require additional exploration?

BT: Yes. At a certain point, the ideas attain a level such that I am no longer interested in exploring them further.

JK: But there is a difference between "I've done it" and "I've done it with such acuity that I do not need to do it again."

BT: You are right. It is important to pursue the exploration until you are honestly satisfied with the results. After La Villette, I will never do a major public park again. With the completion of Marne-la-Vallée and Miami, I may not want to return to the problem of an architecture school again. I certainly do not want to do a student center in a historical setting ever again!

JK: The problem is deeper than program. While you may or may not choose to undertake another school project, you will certainly continue to grapple with the nature of certain building elements and spatial relationships.

Compare Le Fresnoy to Rouen. Both locate a fundamental architectural problem in the simple act of moving through an envelope. This is the kind of problem I am talking about. I would argue that this is a problem that you have not yet fully resolved.

BT: We architects suffer from an unhealthy desire to resolve everything. Take the problem of the corner in classical architecture. There have been thousands of years of experimentation and research, yet still no resolution. An insistence on resolution can be an effective pedagogical tool, but it does not necessarily have to be the ultimate goal. Instead, I wish to push the project far enough that it becomes an inescapable reference point. I would like to see any conversation about a contemporary urban park have to include La Villette, any discussion of small-scale glass construction be incomplete without Groningen.

JK: You must admit that you continue to create situations in which you force yourself to return to a specific problem of entry and work through it in terms of residual space.

BT: Perhaps it is an important problem. Or maybe it is my own limitation.

JK: A critic has to be careful in these situations. The last thing I want to do is make you conscious of the problem and have you stop doing it.

Folly N7, Parc de la Villette

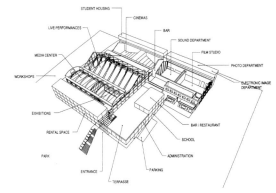

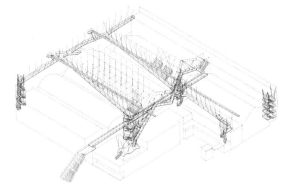

middle and left:
Axonometrics, Le Fresnoy

Top and above: Groningen Video Gallery,
Groningen, Netherlands, 1990

BT: I would like to speak of building envelopes. I prefer to work with envelopes rather than facades, because I want to avoid the historical baggage lodged in the latter term. Facades are nothing more than an aesthetic artifice—a building has no need for them. An envelope, on the other hand, is a necessity. One must provide protection from rain, from weather, from burglars, but this does not oblige us to participate in the arduous task of composing facades.

An enormous body of design theory exists focused upon the composition of facades. When you study this body of work, you'll find that two camps of thinkers emerge: the art historians and the architecture historians. Although I generalize, these two groups employ markedly different approaches. Architecture historians have a tendency to discuss typology. They focus upon the abstract tools of the discipline: plans, sections,

et cetera. In the better cases, the discussion will concentrate upon space, movement, and experience.

The art historians take a different tack. One finds only tertiary discussions of plans and sections, often in terms of figure or symbolism, and much more emphasis upon the composition of facades. They imply that architectural surfaces can be analyzed in the same manner as paintings. I have always felt uneasy about that. I try to avoid making architecture in terms of its figural composition. Instead, I prefer that the visual expression of a building come directly from the materialization of its concept.

I attempt this through a ruthless objectivity and a precise, mechanical technique. In this manner, I am able to avoid traditional design methodologies and the trap of composition. At La Villette, for example, we devised a simple construction game, akin to Lego blocks, in which elements could only be assembled in certain ways. We composed nothing. The instrumental rules of design gave us the visual result.

In the case of Le Fresnoy, the visual image of the project obtained primarily from the existing structures on the site. The architectural surfaces we added were for the most part blank planes that appear to be taken directly from the curtain-wall catalogs. But the result is far from quotidian. We achieve the striking image of the building through a juxtaposition of elements that were rich enough in themselves to give us the result we sought. There was no facade as such, just the end result of a clear methodology.

Our project for a glass pavilion at Groningen provides another example. Here the concept was to push the idea of glass construction to its absolute limit. The transparency and homogeneity of the material precludes any composition of elements. Instead, the ephemeral reflections on the glass activate the surface.

Here is a hypothetical question for architecture students: Have you ever done a project where the exterior comes first? Of course not! We are all good modernists here. The inside always comes first!

If only this were the case. In many projects, this clarity of intention is impossible. Due to any number of factors, many projects begin before the program has been determined. Our project at Lerner Hall at Columbia University is an example. The program was not finalized until we were well into the project. Even when it finally was defined, it proved so generic as to have no impact upon the exterior. We had to design an envelope on its own, with circulation alone driving the design.

But we have seen other architects explore this course before. Take the late work of Mies van der Rohe in Chicago. What lies behind the facades of those towers is of no significance to their development. The intensity of the project is invested entirely within the tectonic investigation. The envelope itself becomes the project.

We spoke earlier of Herzog and de Meuron, another practice that has taken up this sort of exploration and achieved totally different results. They do envelopes; they do not do anything else. The rest of it, the typological way they organize spaces and program, is very restrained. It is clean, controlled, ordered. While I do not personally pursue such a single-minded investigation, I very much respect the work they do.

I am increasingly concerned with this type of problem. Our project for the concert hall at Rouen takes up this investigation as its primary focus.

Lerner Hall Student Center,
Columbia University, New York City, 1994–99

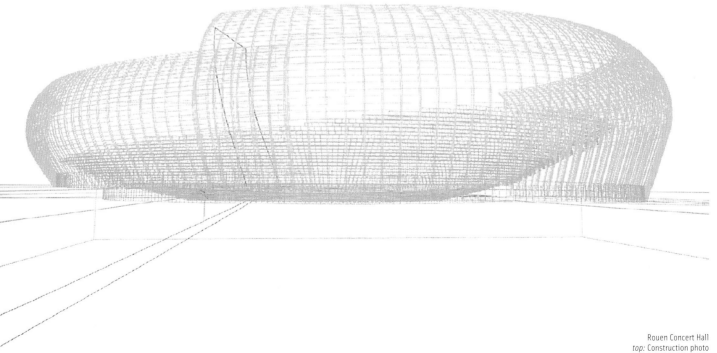

Rouen Concert Hall
top: Construction photo

above: Skin study, with interior seating

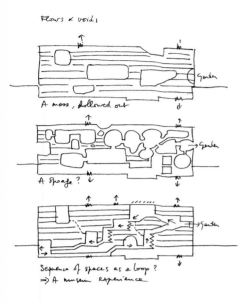

Flows & voids

A mass, hollowed out

A Sponge?

Sequence of spaces as a loop?
=> A museum experience

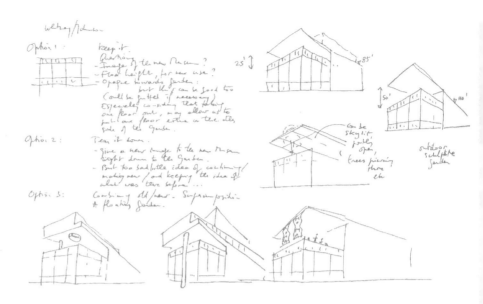

Wittgenstein/...

Option 1:   keep it
- Raising the new Museum?
- Image of the new Museum?
- Float height, for new use?
- Opaque towards garden:
  but they can be good too
  Could be gutted if necessary
  Especially considering that pulling
  one floor out, may allow us to
  pull one floor extra on the other
  side of the Garden.

Option 2:   Tear it down:
- give a new image to the new Museum
  bright down to the Garden.
- But too sad/while idea of containing/
  making new/and keeping the idea of
  what was there before...

Option 3:   Combining old/new - Superposition
  A floating Garden.

25'   85'

50'   180'

Can be
skylit/
partly
open;
trees piercing
through
etc

outdoor
sculpture
garden

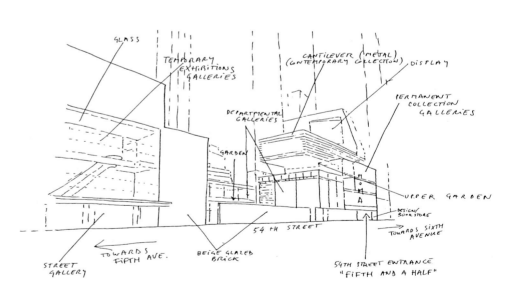

GLASS

TEMPORARY
EXHIBITIONS
GALLERIES

CANTILEVER (METAL)
(CONTEMPORARY COLLECTION)   DISPLAY

DEPARTMENTAL
GALLERIES

PERMANENT
COLLECTION
GALLERIES

GARDEN

UPPER GARDEN

DESIGN/
BOOKSTORE

54TH STREET

TOWARDS SIXTH
AVENUE

TOWARDS
FIFTH AVE.

BEIGE GLAZED
BRICK

54TH STREET ENTRANCE
"FIFTH AND A HALF"

STREET
GALLERY

BT 9/26/97

Preliminary sketches,
MoMA Extension

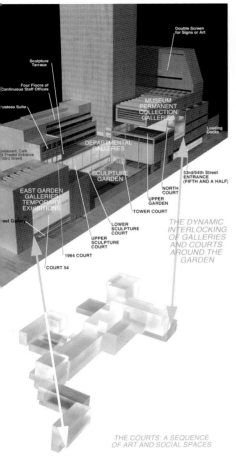

Double Screen
for Signs or Art

Sculpture
Terrace

Four Floors of
Continuous Staff Offices

Trustees Suite

MUSEUM
PERMANENT
COLLECTION
GALLERIES

Restaurant, Café
& Theater Entrance
53rd Street

Loading
Docks

DEPARTMENTAL
GALLERIES

EAST GARDEN
GALLERIES
TEMPORARY
EXHIBITIONS

SCULPTURE
GARDEN

53rd/54th Street
ENTRANCE
(FIFTH AND A HALF)

eet Gallery

NORTH
COURT

UPPER
GARDEN

TOWER COURT

LOWER
SCULPTURE
COURT

*THE DYNAMIC
INTERLOCKING
OF GALLERIES
AND COURTS
AROUND THE
GARDEN*

UPPER
SCULPTURE
COURT

1964 COURT

COURT 54

*THE COURTS: A SEQUENCE
OF ART AND SOCIAL SPACES*

BT: I'll preface our discussion of Rouen with a short description of the competition we did for the expansion of the MoMA in New York. This was a huge project that consumed the office for an entire summer. We threw ourselves into the work with abandon. The project, I feel, was quite strong. But beyond that . . . you cannot imagine the politics involved! The process was very public, we knew the jury, we knew all of the competitors very well (the finalists, in addition to our office, included Steven Holl, Rem Koolhaas, Herzog and de Meuron and Yoshio Taniguchi). We, of course, knew their work and could imagine what they might propose . . .

We followed it all! We knew who was having dinner with whom, who was playing golf, everything. In addition, there were the personal apprehensions I alluded to in another conversation about what winning would mean for the future of the office.

We all know the outcome: Taniguchi was awarded the commission. This loss created an incredible void in the office and a certain degree of cynicism with regard to the work.

Soon after, we were invited to do a competition for a large seven-thousand-seat auditorium in Rouen. In a sense, we treated the project as a kind of cathartic recovery following the political intensity of MoMA. Here we would simply do what we wanted. No politics, no compromises. We would simply come up with as strong an entry as we could—that's it.

Competition renderings, MoMA Extension

We did the competition with just two team members in one month's time. I did not know who the other competitors were. I did not know the jury. It was a complete reversal of the MoMA strategy: we went in blind and were chosen. The project was built in just thirteen months—before Taniguchi had begun the foundations at MoMA! Of course, I am very happy with this project.

TG: How could you produce the project so quickly?

We had strong preliminary work behind us in an unbuilt competition for an urban intervention in Chartres, where we had already explored an auditorium of similar size and scope. Although I believe we achieved a focused conceptual idea with that project, we never had the opportunity to work out the tectonic implications. It seemed only natural to take those initial ideas that we felt strongly about and develop them further in Rouen.

It is tempting to say that we simply recycled the Chartres proposal, but that would not be accurate. Up until Rouen, the discussion had centered on dissociation and fragmentation, on programmatic and spatial disjunctions. At Rouen, the notion of the abstract envelope became the key concept.

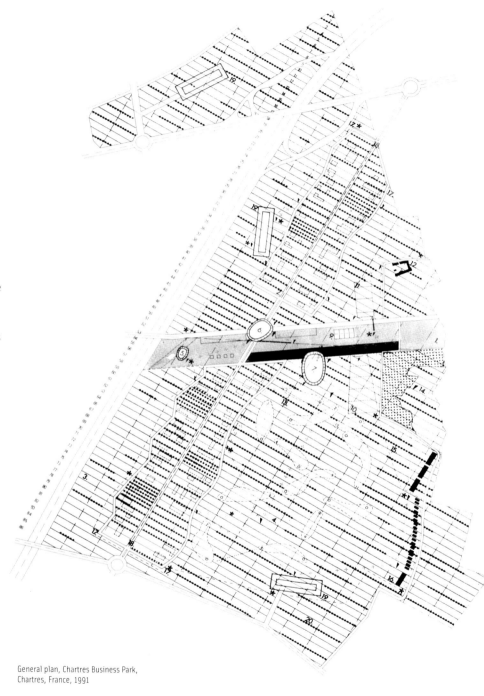

General plan, Chartres Business Park,
Chartres, France, 1991

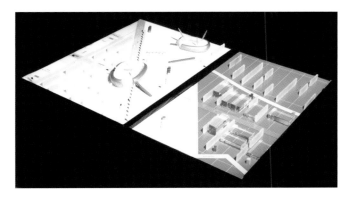

Chartres Business Park
top: Model of movement strategies

middle: Rendering

above: Curved hall rendering

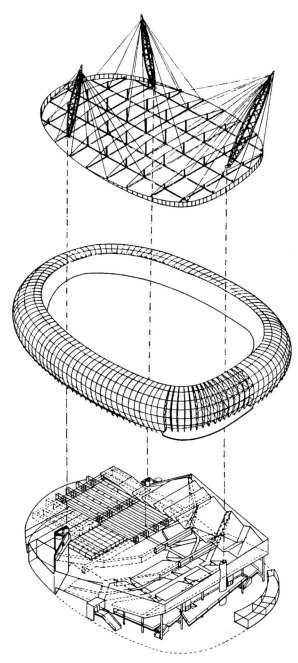

Three curved halls similar construction
accommodate varied amenities

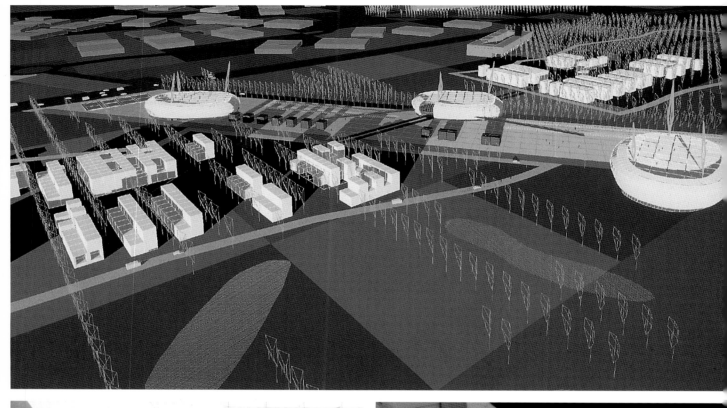

Chartres Business Park
top: Aerial perspective

left: Skin study

opposite top: Aerial perspective

opposite bottom: Views of model

JK: Could we say that MoMA represents the last of the programmatic investigations and Rouen the first of the constructional investigations?

BT: In terms of what we have built, I would say you are correct, but in truth, the trajectory was not so black and white. These ideas had been percolating in earlier projects for some time, and the programmatic interests have not entirely disappeared.

TG: Clearly the hybrid tendencies of the building, both programmatically and structurally, were a part of the investigation from the beginning. Could you expand?

BT: We have done quite a bit of work for public entities, so for us, budget is always a concern. Large spans, in the case of Rouen over three hundred feet, cost a lot of money. By using the hybrid system of masts and tensile cables, we were able to create individual spans of one third the total span, which required much shallower trusses. Shallower trusses mean less steel; less steel means less money.

But, of course, the decision is not entirely pragmatic. Both Chartres and Rouen were situated near major highways, and it was important that both projects have a strong visual presence to passing motorists. The height of the masts gives us that presence. At night, when they are lit, the building can be seen from an incredible distance.

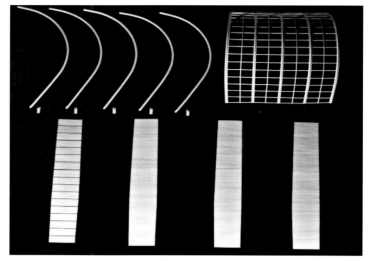

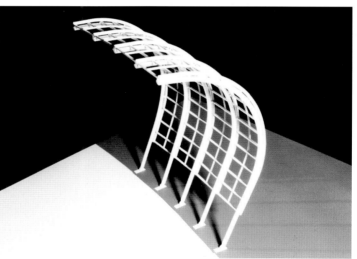

Chartres Business Park
top and above: Torus and skin studies

Interior rendering, Chartres Business Park

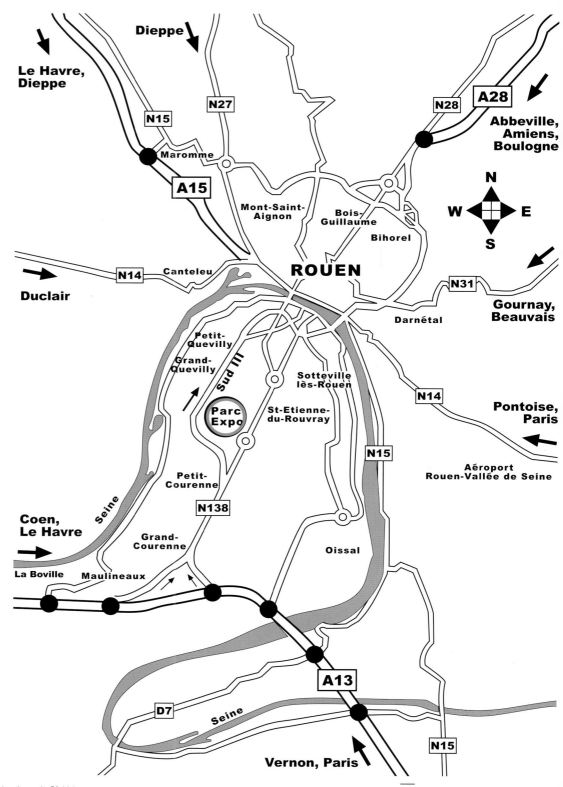

Rouen and environs: the Zénith is
located at Parc Expo.

TG: The site at Rouen was formerly used as an airfield. Was this fact of any significance to the project?

BT: The notion of the airfield had absolutely no role in the conception of the project. I remain terribly suspicious of any architecture that uses referentiality as a mode of justification. For instance, I could say that the red of the *folies* at Le Parc de la Villette is in reference to the blood of the abattoirs, but it would be totally false. That is why I have always answered, "Because red is not a color."

I do not do meaning in architecture.

JK: Theoretically, we can understand why. Any text lends itself to readings regardless of what was intended simply because of the capacity of any frame to support meaning.

BT: Of course. I do not wish to condition the creation; I only devise the conditions. I have no problem with others, reading meaning into the projects, but it is never my aim to direct the course of those readings. I am far more interested in producing a work upon which visitors can project their own interpretations, fantasies, and obsessions.

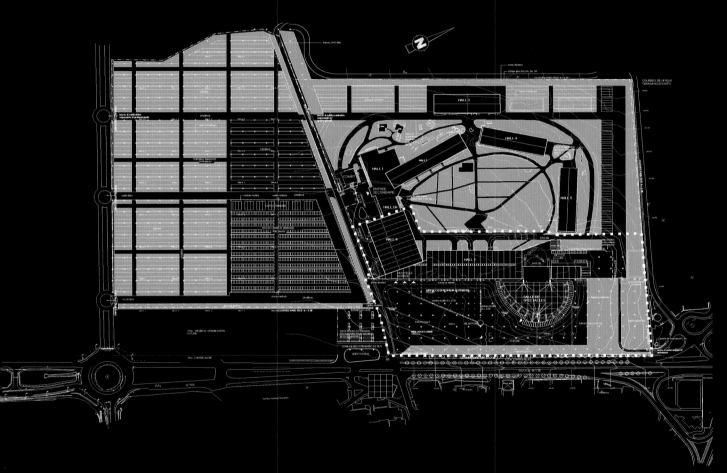

Site plan

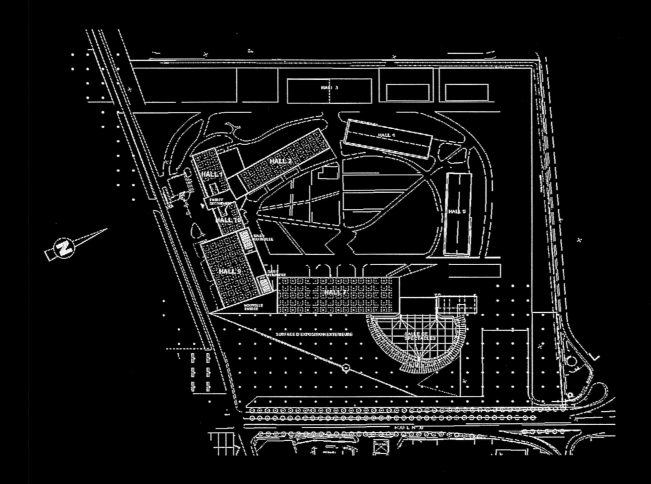

Area of halls
Hall 1
Surface   1530m2
Surface stands   504m2

Hall 2
Surface   3,000m2
Surface stands   1296m2

Hall 7
Surface   6,000m2
Surface Stands   2646m2

Hall 9
Surface   3,780m2
Surface stands   1,620m2

Hall 10
Surface   800m2
Surface stands   288m2

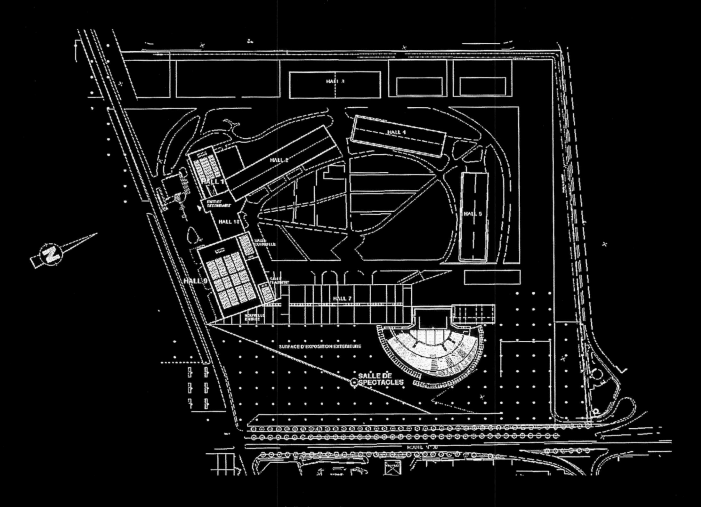

Auditorium capacity
Main concert hall   5,424 persons

Hall 1   1,152 persons
Hall 9   3,500 persons
Corneille room   320 persons
Flaubert room   192 persons

Total   10,588 persons
(Maximum allowable)

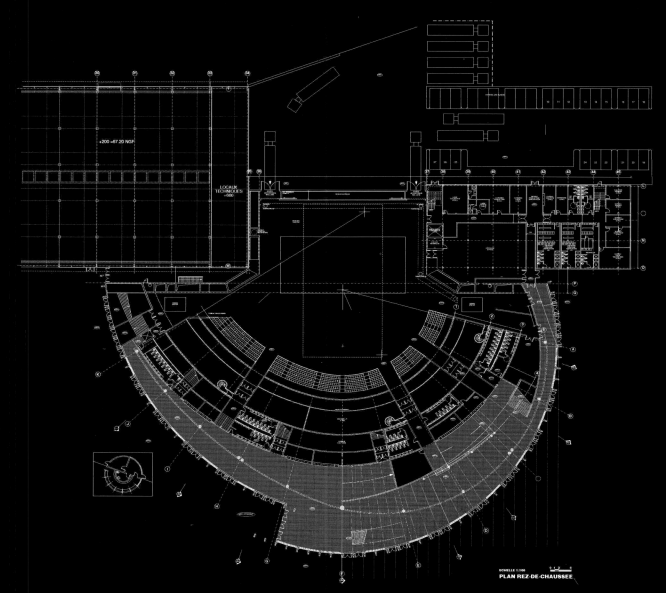

ECHELLE 1:100
PLAN REZ-DE-CHAUSSEE

Plan 000

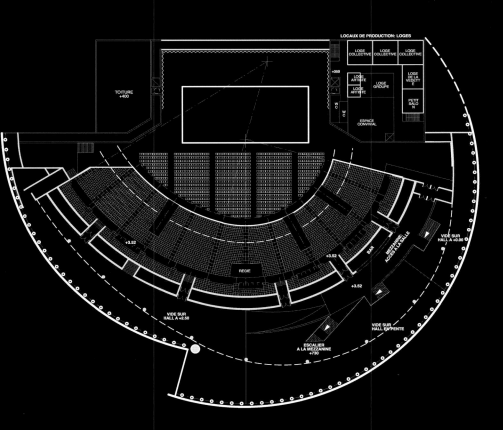

LOCAUX DE PRODUCTION: LOGES

| LOGE COLLECTIVE | LOGE COLLECTIVE | LOGE COLLECTIVE |

+350

TOITURE
+400

LOGE ARTISTE
LOGE ARTISTE
W C
W C

LOGE GROUPE

LOGE DE LA VEDETTE

PETIT SALON

ESPACE CONVIVIAL

+3.52

REGIE

+3.52

+3.52

BAR

MEZZANINE
ACCES A LA SALLE

VIDE SUR
HALL A +0.00

VIDE SUR
HALL A +2.50

VIDE SUR
HALL EN PENTE

ESCALIER
A LA MEZZANINE
+730

Plan +400

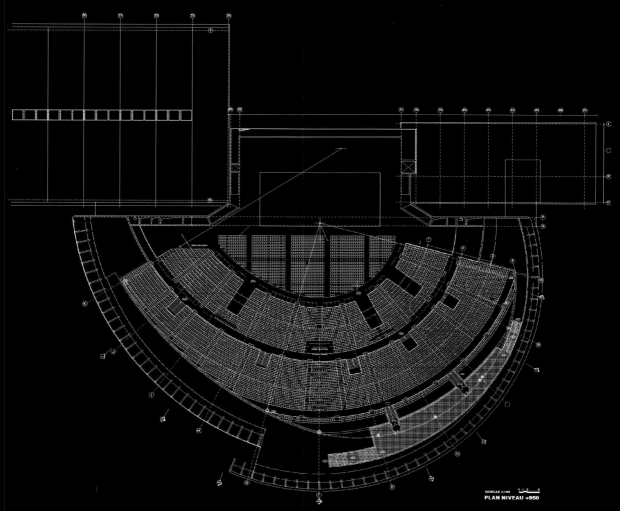

PLAN NIVEAU +950

Plan +950

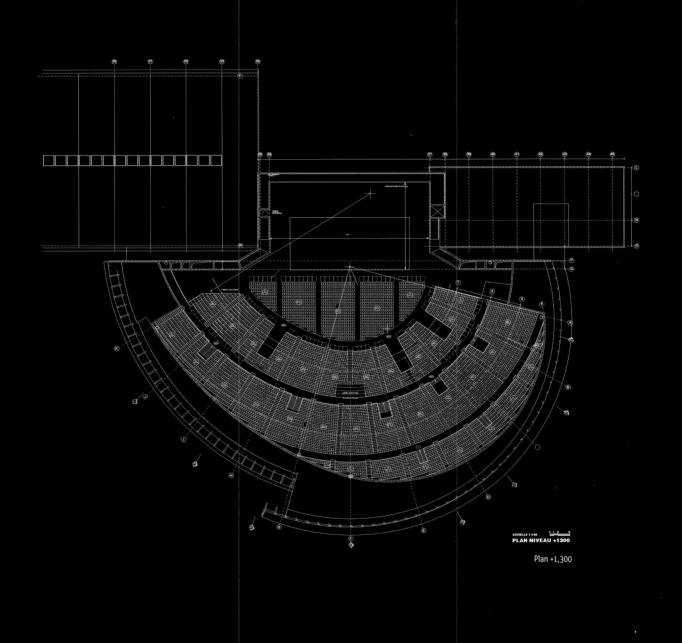

ECHELLE 1:100
PLAN NIVEAU +1300

Plan +1,300

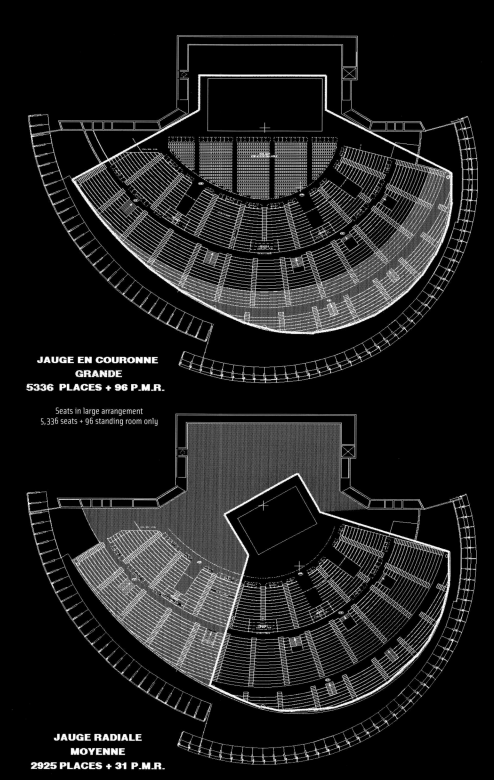

**JAUGE EN COURONNE
GRANDE
5336 PLACES + 96 P.M.R.**

Seats in large arrangement
5,336 seats + 96 standing room only

**JAUGE RADIALE
MOYENNE
2925 PLACES + 31 P.M.R.**

Seats in average radial
2,925 seats + 96 standing room only

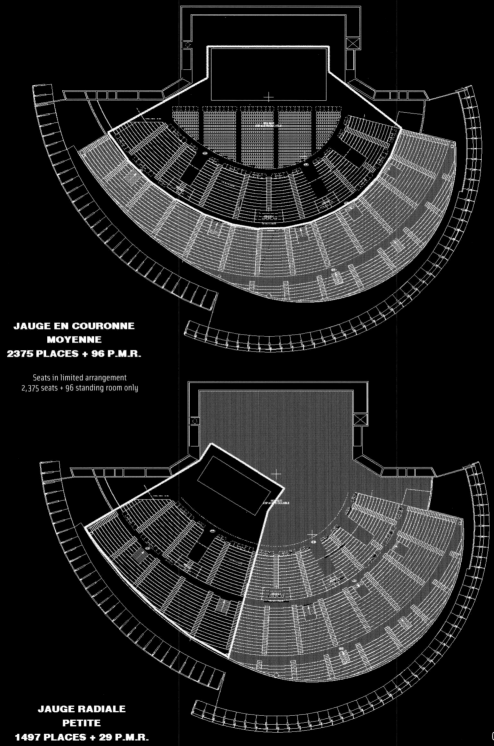

**JAUGE EN COURONNE
MOYENNE
2375 PLACES + 96 P.M.R.**

Seats in limited arrangement
2,375 seats + 96 standing room only

**JAUGE RADIALE
PETITE
1497 PLACES + 29 P.M.R.**

Seats in small radial
1,497 seats + 29 standing room only

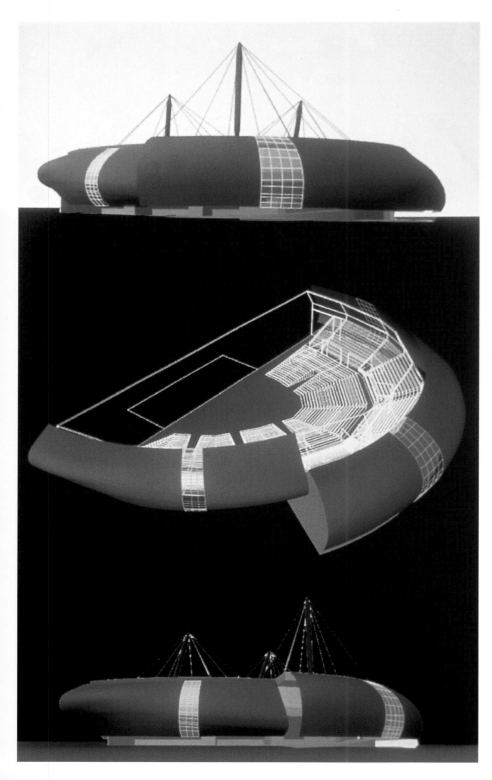

Concert hall renderings

View from highway (computer rendering)

TG: Tell us more about the development of the envelope at Rouen.

BT: Acoustical requirements confirmed our intuition of the double envelope. The noise level within the concert hall itself will climb to over one hundred twenty decibels, while the city codes allow only thirty-five decibels on the exterior. The layers of building surfaces act as baffles to reduce the transfer of noise between interior and exterior.

This space between the two skins becomes the conceptual nexus of the project. Within this space, the movement of the visitors sculpts the interior space in a manner akin to the spatial carvings I explored in the *Manhattan Transcripts*. The transition structure above solves the complex intersection of the outer wall and the roof structure while simultaneously allowing the interstitial space to continue vertically through the project.

But one question remained. How does one enter a hermetic, homogenous surface? How does one enter a football? Our solution here was to create an incision and simply pull it apart.

I wanted to separate the two skins so that visually one could identify the differences between them. In a sense, pulling them apart provides, in effect, a giant negative reveal; it is the point in the structure that provides a way to reinforce the concept.

TG: This, to me, marks a crucial departure from the earlier projects. At both Le Fresnoy and Chartres the visitor slides underneath the skin.

BT: But at Le Fresnoy you don't really have a problem, because the roof never fully encloses the complex. At Chartres, the problem of entry was never fully explored. We handled it in a fairly typical manner: we simply come in from below.

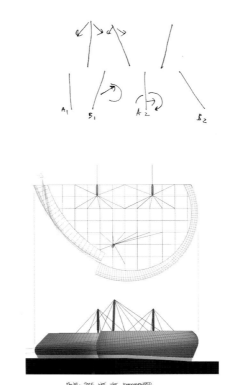

Mast and stage strategies

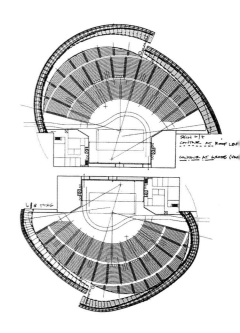

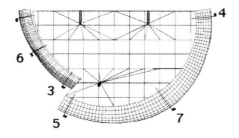

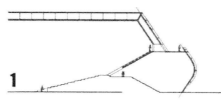

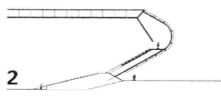

TG: Early section drawings through the wall exhibit a complexity that does not carry into the realized project. Can you tell us more about the development of the torus profile?

BT: There is an enormous difference between the questions you ask yourself at the level of a competition and the questions you ask when the commission is secured. The strategy is simple: win the competition, then explore the possibilities. In order to win, it is imperative that the submission clearly illustrates the concept. If you win the competition, you can go back and explore all the possibilities that the concept entails. The competition process is all about focus, but once you've won, you have the liberty to allow the project to go out of focus a bit in order to play out all of the possibilities.

Here we were indulging in just this kind of exploration. The complex shapes were eventually rejected in order to avoid formal self-indulgence.

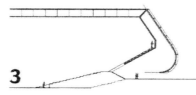

JK: How much time does this exploration consume?

BT: Perhaps a period of two to three weeks.

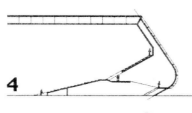

JK: I have difficulty with these drawings, because each constitutes a distinct architectural proposition. They all explore the complex relationships between the volume, the person, and the ground.

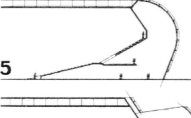

BT: But you must remember these do not represent alternatives or options. They are more like a movie sequence, showing section cuts at regular intervals, sequentially. Along the periphery of the building, the interior space would change dramatically with these inflections. It was to have been a fluid transformation from one to the next. But in the end, we were not interested in that kind of sculptural effect.

Preliminary sections

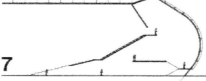

Our decision to reject this line of investigation was made in order to protect the integrity of the building's concept: the idea of orchestrating movement in the space between the two skins. If the envelope was allowed to become too complicated, eventually it would compete with the spatial ideas for attention. In my work the performative aspects will always take precedence over aesthetic concerns.

For these same reasons, you will notice that the fenestration in the earlier schemes is simplified greatly in the final work. We did not want the project to reduce itself to a graphic exercise.

TG: Did economics come into play here? All of these decisions seem to favor the less costly alternative.

BT: Clearly we are happy when a decision produces an economic benefit, but we do not allow that to drive the project. Certainly the simpler envelope allowed us to complete the project within the budgetary and time constraints we were faced with.

This is not to say that what was built did not pose its own challenges. By standardizing the profile of the skin, the contractors could fabricate a series of identical components. In the inflected scheme, we would have had to produce each piece individually—a significant expense on a project of this size. We find that contractors do not possess the tools we architects do. To realize the project, one has to devise a standardized system that can achieve the desired effect.

Model detail of interior

Model views

JK: I want to interject a question. I'll begin with an observation of what seems to me to be a theoretical fissure. I would outline it as follows: the early work was guided by a deep suspicion of architecture as autonomous practice—the possibility that a significant building could develop from a set of ideas internal to the discourse of architecture.

In response, you introduced interdisciplinarity as a means of broadening the discourse, a technique we can trace from the *Transcripts* to the MoMA competition.

Now, when I hear you speak of hybrid structural systems and the profile of the envelope, it sounds as if you are beginning to see architecture in exactly the kind of autonomous role you initially set out to criticize. You now describe the adequacy of a project to take up the discourse without resorting to outside theory. Would that be fair to say?

BT: The suspicion and the critical outlook of the early work coincided with an intensely urban attitude. Actual fragmentation became a means to bring the qualities of the city into the project itself. If you were to look at our project for the Tokyo Opera, for example, you would see a series of disassociated bands juxtaposed to each other in an organization that in a very real sense is extended into the fabric of the city. La Villette is another example. In these projects our intent was solely to activate space. There was no boundary between inside and outside. In fact, there was really no boundary between the built work and the drawings.

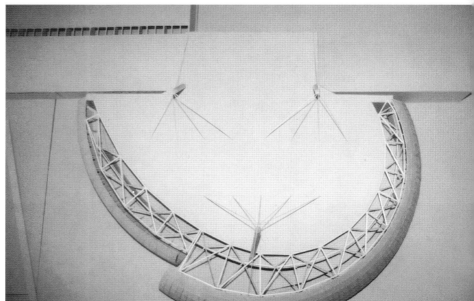

Model views
top: View of ramp

above: Roof

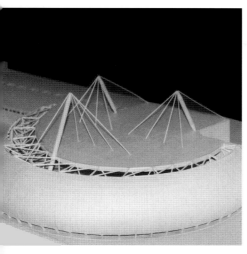

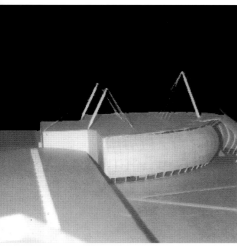

This methodology cannot be employed in every project. In much of our more recent work, we are confronted with constantly shifting building programs. Under these circumstances, the idea of the envelope must precede the resolution of the program.

There are two very basic issues at play: enclosure and movement. In the early work movement was always in relation to activated spaces but rarely in relation to the architecture itself. There was a determination to extend the effects of the projects as widely as possible. In the more recent work, the development of the envelope provides us a mechanism to engage the architecture itself more aggressively.

Our project at Le Fresnoy marks an important moment in the development of these ideas. The project comprises a series of found objects upon which we superimposed a large roof. The space between the large roof and the objects it covers marks the beginning of an incredible discovery. This strategy of placing objects in unorthodox relationships can actually replace composition as a design technique. It is every bit as powerful as the graphic juxtapositions we explored in the early theoretical projects. The technique was developed further at Chartres and again in a more structured manner at Rouen. The programmatic issues are no longer needed to drive the design. It is simply a matter of coordinating movement within and through the envelope.

General views

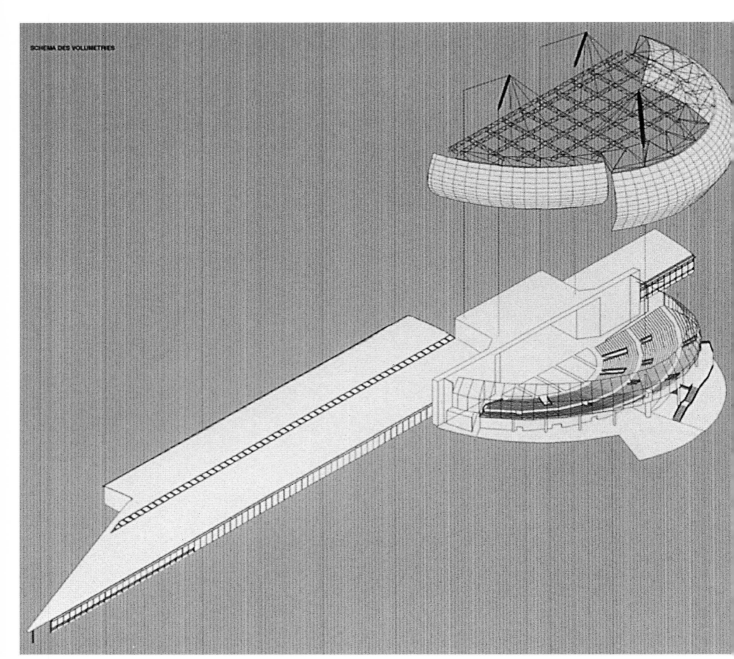

SCHEMA DES VOLUMETRES

Overview

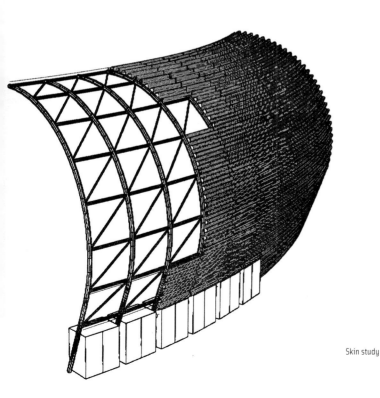

JK: Perhaps I can establish a trajectory. In the *Transcripts* you interrupt the categorical typologies of the conventional in architecture. By playing the sprocket holes in film against classical dentil molding, for example, a device that belongs to two separate disciplines is essentially constructed and deconstructed at the same time. It becomes visually impossible to say whether something is a building or building language.

At Le Fresnoy, the technique becomes more sophisticated. We inhabit the roofscape of traditional buildings, the new roof doubles as a screen for projection, the old roofs no longer perform conventional sheltering tasks. All these are devices that once again interrupt the categorical expectations of architectural elements.

At Rouen we see an even deeper sophistication. Here one needs to know enough about architecture to know that the transition from roof to wall across the torus shape is significant. That hybridization of elements is likely to go unnoticed by the uninitiated. I am arguing that you are becoming increasingly willing to allow these disruptions to occur entirely within an architectural intelligence. Would you agree?

BT: Yes, your analysis is correct. But I must reiterate that the word *architecture* must be understood as the act of combining movement and spaces, not as the history or the art of architecture. And we must not forget materiality.

Skin study

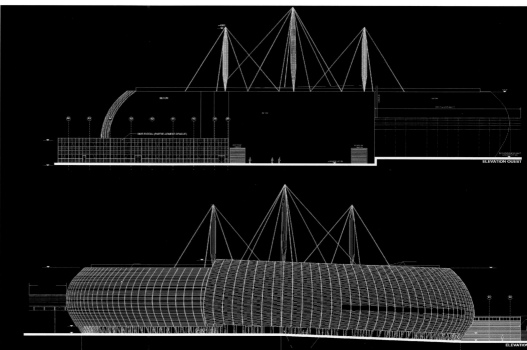

top: Corridor study

above: Elevations

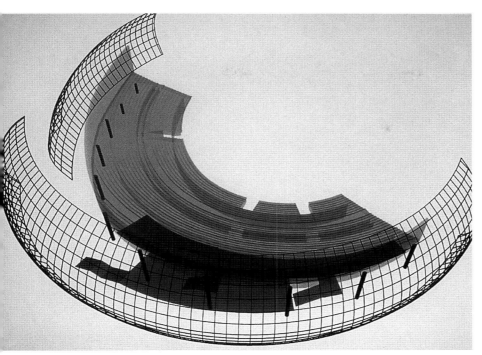

It takes a long time to understand how to build things. When I did La Villette, perhaps even at Le Fresnoy, I had no idea how to put buildings together. I literally learned on the job.

Perhaps a more important building in terms of this transition would be the school of architecture at Marne-la-Vallée. Here I was trying to learn about everything: concrete, steel, glass, wood. So much was going on that I fear we lost some of the conceptual precision. The fact that only the first phase was built does not help . . .

At Rouen that conceptual precision returns. Here we employ just three materials: concrete, steel, and glass. Indeed the reason for the transparent seats was to avoid the addition of another material; visually they operate like glass.

TG: So by tightening the palette of materials you were actually able to increase the range of effects.

BT: Exactly. But in order to achieve that tectonic simplicity, we had to overcome an incredible number of technical constraints. We were lucky to be able to do it.

It is important to make the clients a part of the process. If they do not understand the concept, you risk losing it all. The next thing you know you'll have a little carpet here, a chandelier there, a little of this, a little of that . . . You must really work to maintain a material ruthlessness.

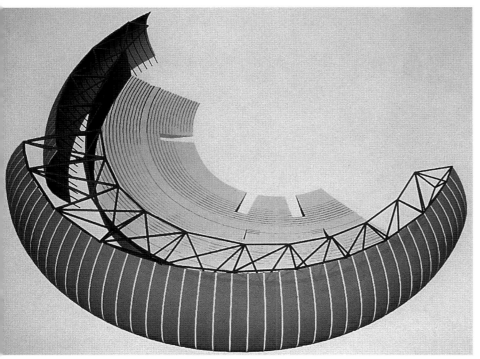

top and above: Envelope studies

ROVEN SHELL GEOMETRY.

PROFILE SEGMENT 1	≠	PROFILE SEGMENT 2
RADIUS	≠	RADIUS
AXIS	≠	AXIS

AXIS 1 + AXIS 2 ARE COPLANAR ~~AND~~ PARALLEL AND

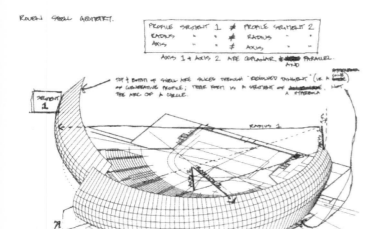

TOP + BOTTOM OF SHELL ARE SLICES THROUGH "REVOLVED TANGENT" (IE A ~~LINE~~ OF GENERATIVE PROFILE; THERE FORM IS A SEGMENT OF ~~ELLIPSE~~, NOT THE ARC OF A CIRCLE.

SEGMENT 1

RADIUS 1

SEGMENT 2

BOTH AXIS 1 + 2 ARE COPLANAR TO FORM PLANE OF ENTRY GLASS.

ROVEN SHELL GEOMETRY.

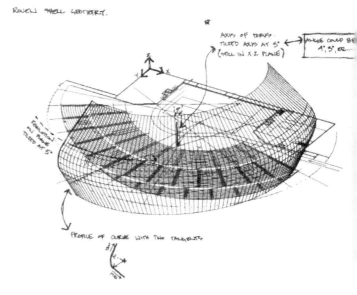

AXIS OF TORUS. TILTED AXIS AT 5° (STILL IN X·Z PLANE)

ANGLE COULD BE 1°, 5°, OR...

PROFILE OF CURVE WITH TWO TANGENTS

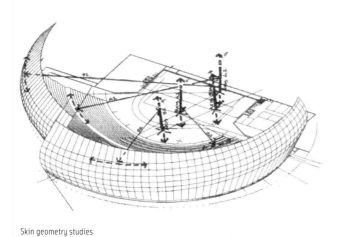

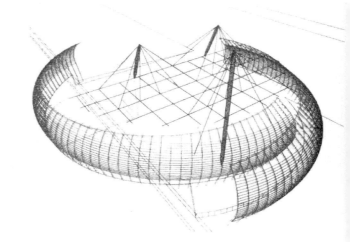

Skin geometry studies

The act of building has made me keenly aware of the conceptual possibilities inherent in construction. Structural and material investigations provide yet another opportunity to develop a concept without resorting to the mediation of architectural history.

JK: It is interesting to me that you think of this project as seminal, it is both psychologically seminal, and a refinement of your own working methods in construction. You were able to tighten the referential field yet maintain the integrity of the discourse.

BT: This is possible only because the building is assembled with a clear conceptual and material strategy. The program itself is simple. The diversity comes in the tension between the envelope, the movement through, and, of course, the crowds.

Although the focus of my work has shifted from the days of the *Transcripts,* I feel that the earlier conceptual preoccupations are still implicit in the current period. The semantic dissociations remain integral to the work. Ultimately I would say that I am still doing the same project, but with different priorities.

JK: If we can show the project in its naked detail and make that point, then we really will have accomplished what we are trying to do.

top: View of entry hall

above: View of entry

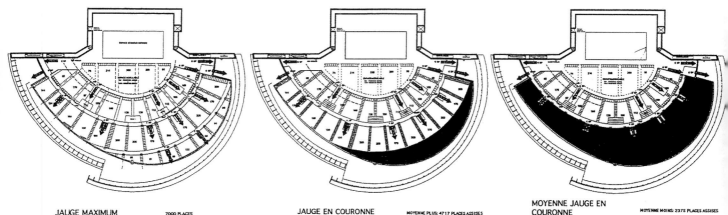

JAUGE MAXIMUM

DEGAGEMENT

PROJET	REGLEMENT
15 SORTIES	15 SORTIES
71 U.P.	70 U.P.

7000 PLACES

DONT 96 P.M.R.

CONFIGURATION ASSIS + DEBOUT:
4422 PLACES ASSISES EN GRADIN
2578 PLACES DEBOUT DANS L'ESPACE MODULABLE

CONFIGURATION ASSIS:
5346 PLACES ASSISES EN GRADIN ET DANS L'ESPACE MODULABLE

Maximum capacity

JAUGE EN COURONNE

DEGAGEMENT

PROJET	REGLEMENT
13 SORTIES	10 SORTIES
65 U.P.	40 U.P.

MOYENNE PLUS: 4717 PLACES ASSISES

DONT 96 P.M.R.

SELON LE NOMBRE DE DEGAGEMENT PREVU DANS CETTE CONFIGURATION, UN MAXIMUM DE 1283 PERSONNES DEBOUT POURRAIT OCCUPER L'ESPACE MODULABLE

Balcony capacity

MOYENNE JAUGE EN COURONNE

DEGAGEMENT

PROJET	REGLEMENT
13 SORTIES	7 SORTIES
65 U.P.	26 U.P.

MOYENNE MOINS: 2375 PLACES ASSISES

DONT 96 P.M.R.

SELON LE NOMBRE DE DEGAGEMENTS PREVU DANS CETTE CONFIGURATION, UN MAXIMUM DE 3625 PERSONNES DEBOUT POURRAIT OCCUPER L'ESPACE MODULABLE

Average capacity in balcony

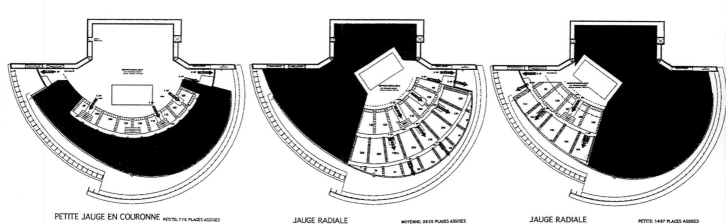

PETITE JAUGE EN COURONNE

PETITE: 776 PLACES ASSISES

DEGAGEMENT

PROJET	REGLEMENT
6 SORTIES	3 SORTIES
27 U.P.	9 U.P.

DONT 46 P.M.R.

SELON LE NOMBRE DE DEGAGEMENTS PREVU DANS CETTE CONFIGURATION, UN MAXIMUM DE 1726 PERSONNES DEBOUT POURRAIT OCCUPER L'ESPACE MODULABLE

Small-balcony capacity

Stage configurations

JAUGE RADIALE
(EVT. SOUS-DIVISION EN COURONNE)

DEGAGEMENT

PROJET	REGLEMENT
9 SORTIES	8 SORTIES
46 U.P.	30 U.P.

MOYENNE: 2926 PLACES ASSISES

DONT 31 P.M.R.

SELON LE NOMBRE DE DEGAGEMENTS PREVU DANS CETTE CONFIGURATION, UN MAXIMUM DE 1875 PERSONNES DEBOUT POURRAIT OCCUPER L'ESPACE MODULABLE

Small stage #1

JAUGE RADIALE
(EVT. SOUS-DIVISION EN COURONNE)

DEGAGEMENT

PROJET	REGLEMENT
5 SORTIES	5 SORTIES
25 U.P.	16 U.P.

PETITE: 1497 PLACES ASSISES

DONT 29 P.M.R.

SELON LE NOMBRE DE DEGAGEMENTS PREVU DANS CETTE CONFIGURATION, UN MAXIMUM DE 503 PERSONNES DEBOUT POURRAIT OCCUPER L'ESPACE MODULABLE

Small stage #2

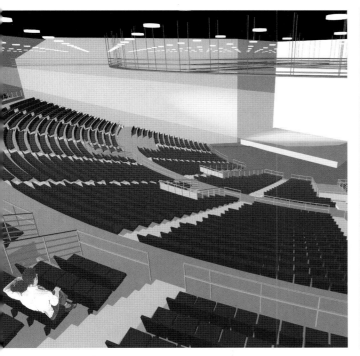

top: Small stage #2

above: Small stage #1

top and above: Views at maximum capacity

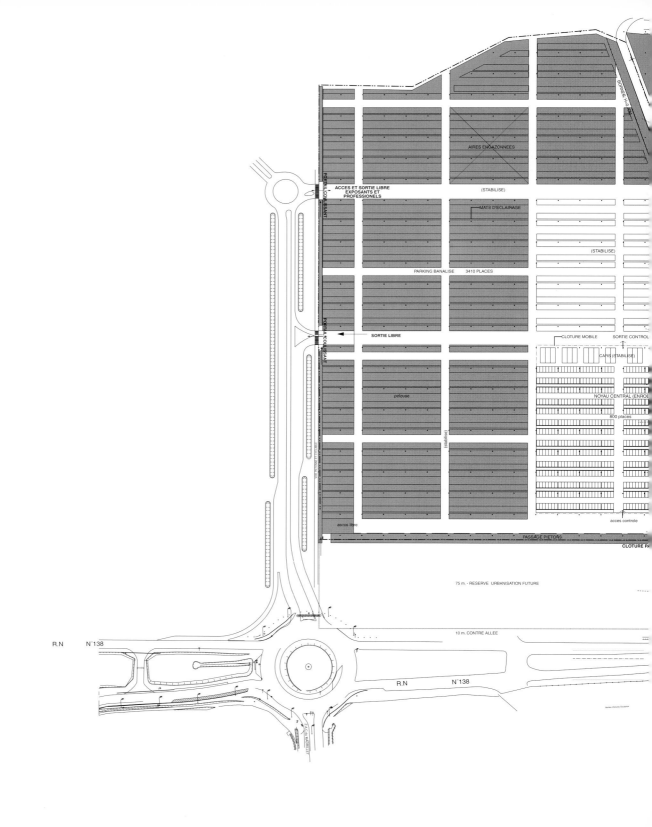

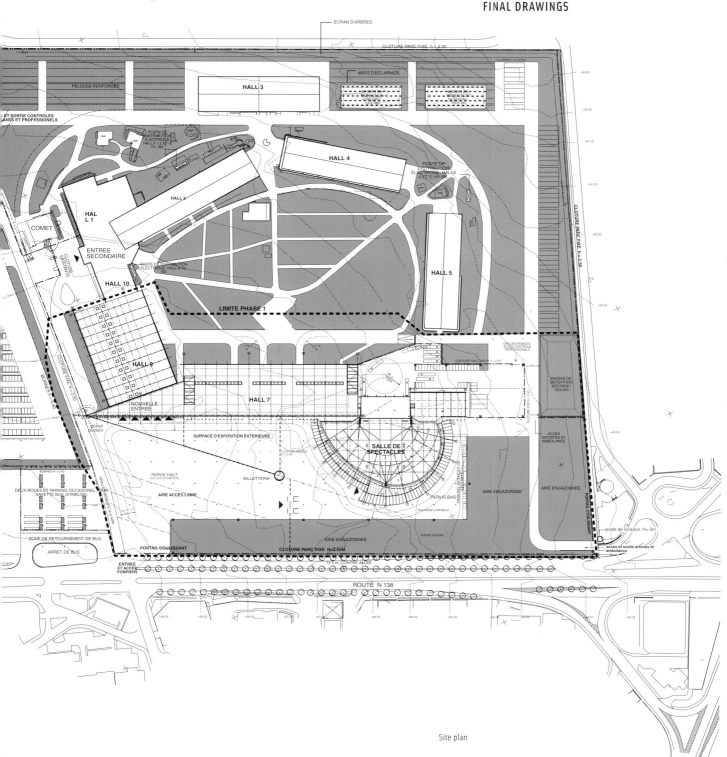

Site plan

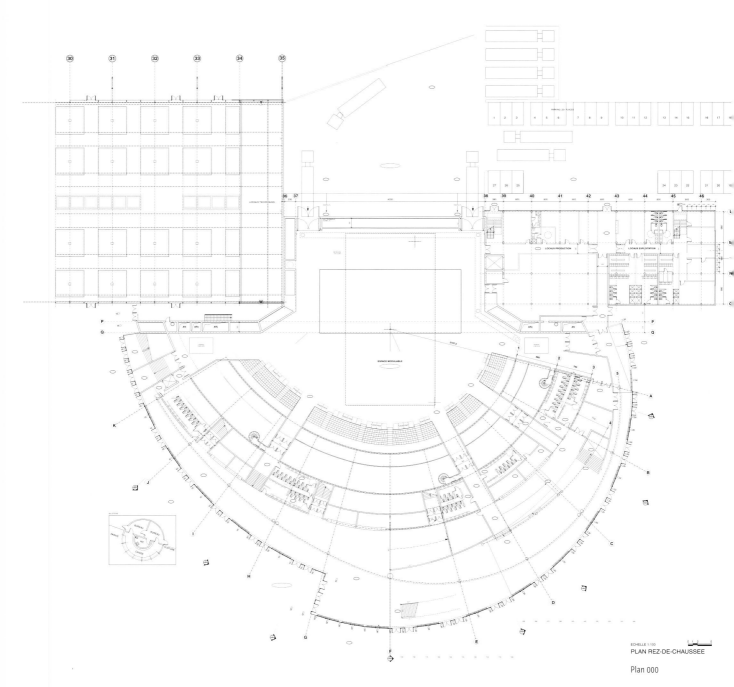

ECHELLE 1:100
PLAN REZ-DE-CHAUSSEE

Plan 000

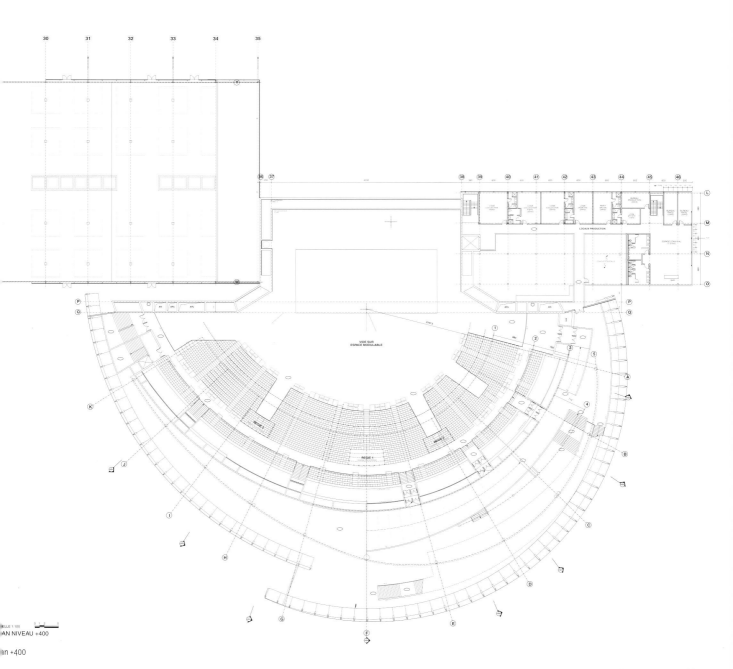

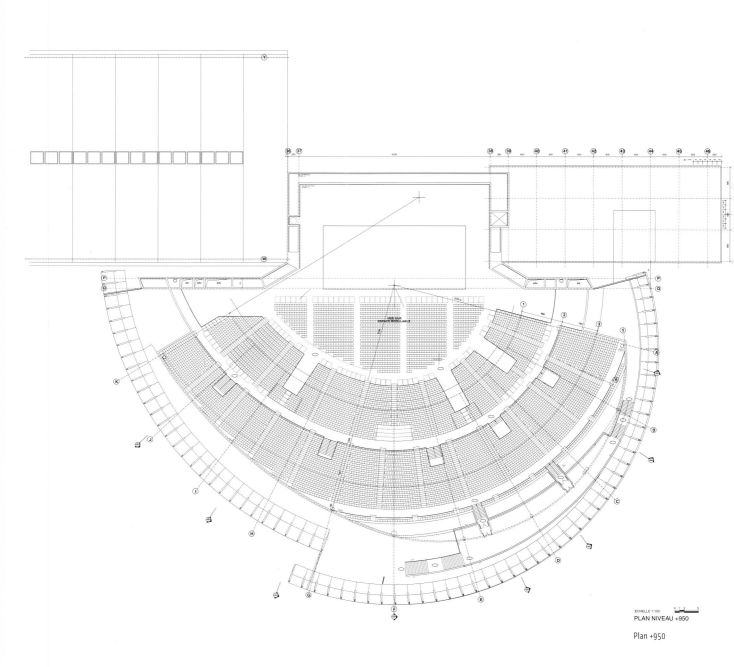

ECHELLE 1:100

PLAN NIVEAU +950

Plan +950

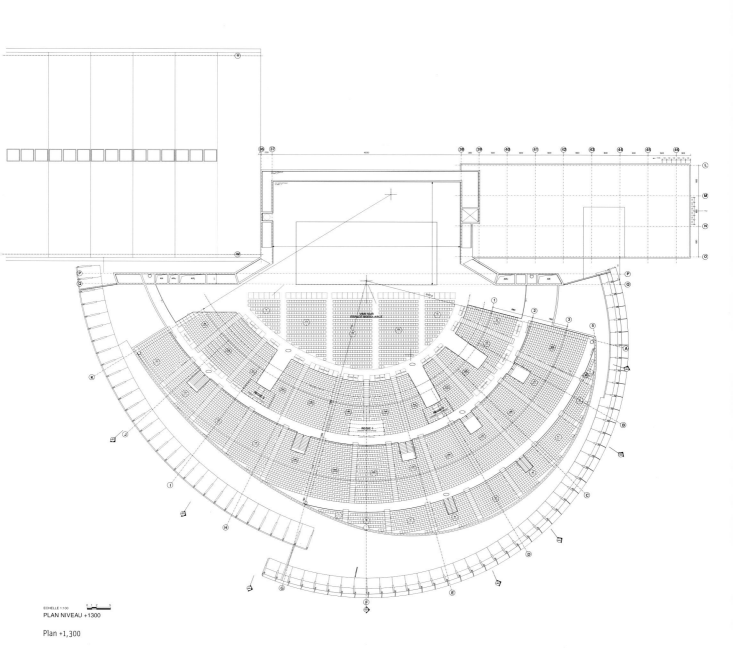

ECHELLE 1:100
PLAN NIVEAU +1300

Plan +1,300

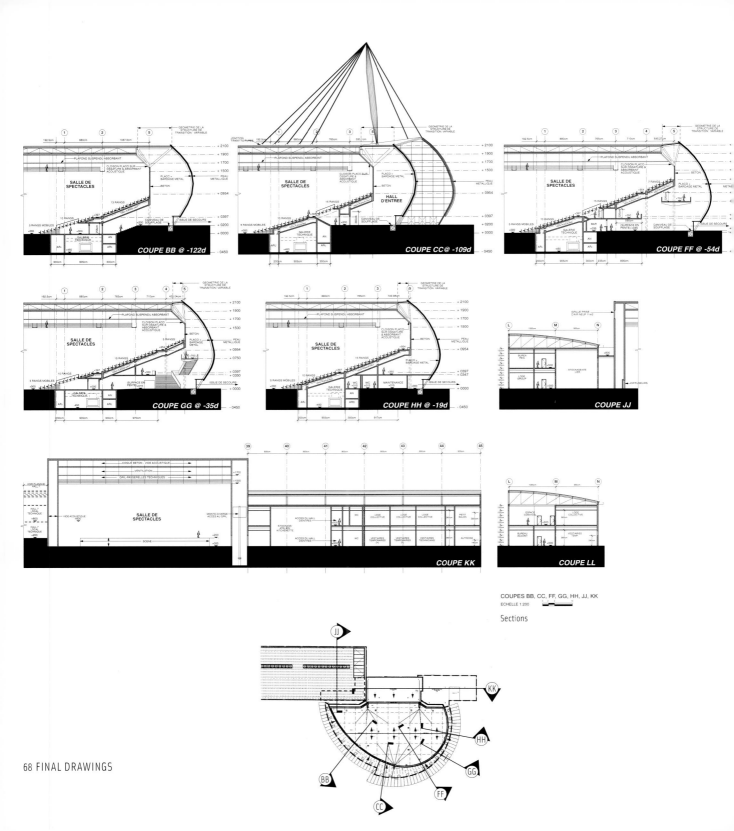

COUPE BB @ -122d

COUPE CC @ -109d

COUPE FF @ -54d

COUPE GG @ -35d

COUPE HH @ -19d

COUPE JJ

COUPE KK

COUPE LL

COUPES BB, CC, FF, GG, HH, JJ, KK
ECHELLE 1:200

Sections

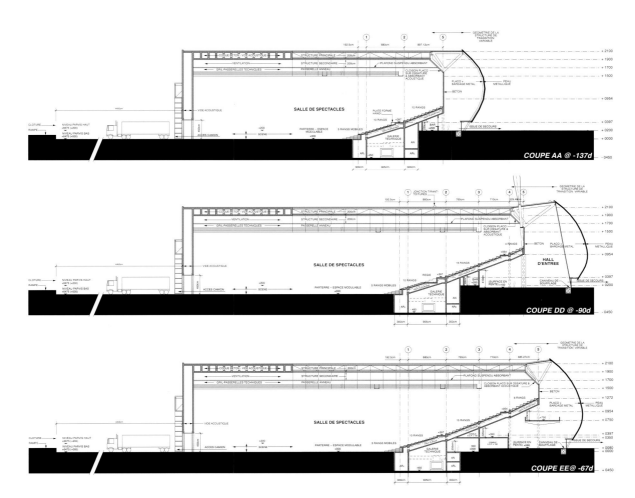

COUPE AA @ -137d

COUPE DD @ -90d

COUPE EE@ -67d

COUPES AA, DD, EE
ECHELLE 1:200

Sections

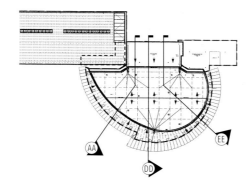

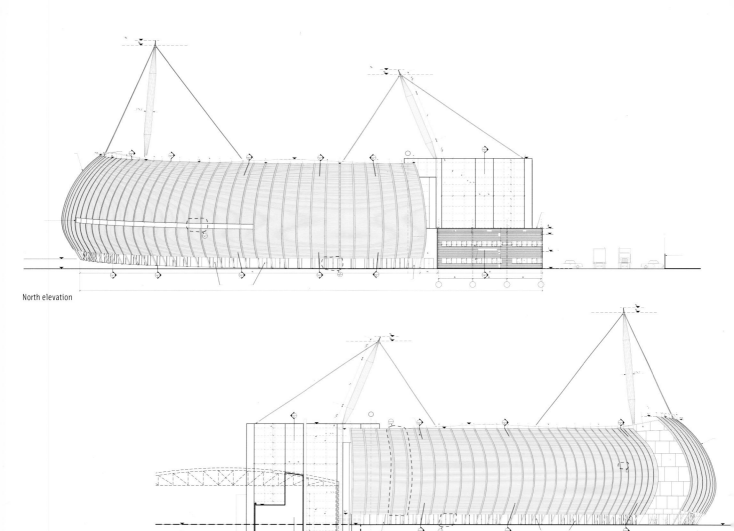

North elevation

South elevation

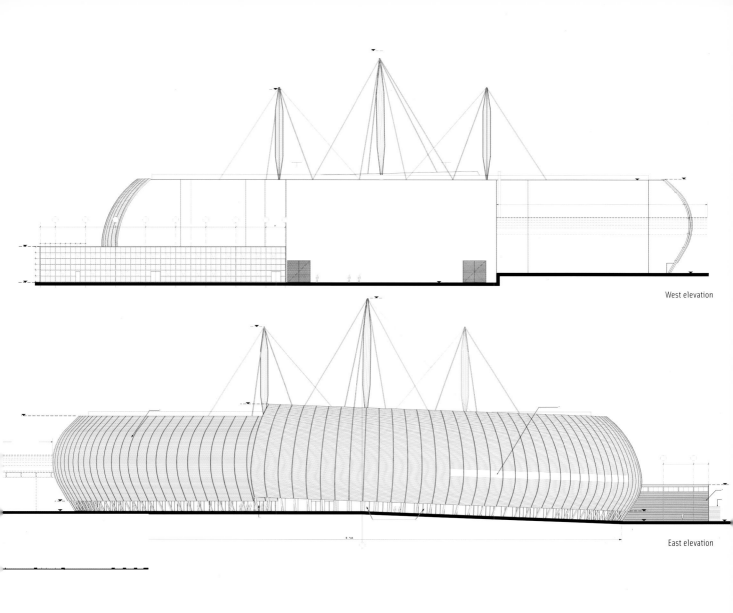

West elevation

East elevation

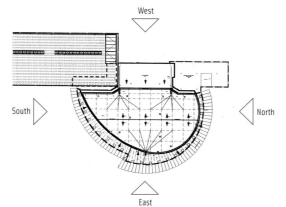

West

South

North

East

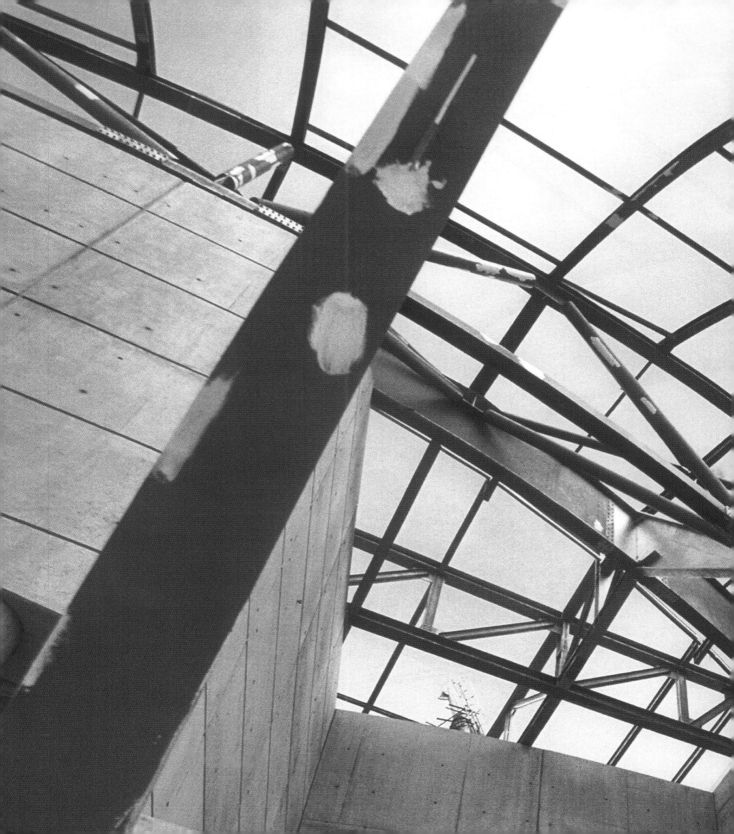

Seating

Transition structure

Skin

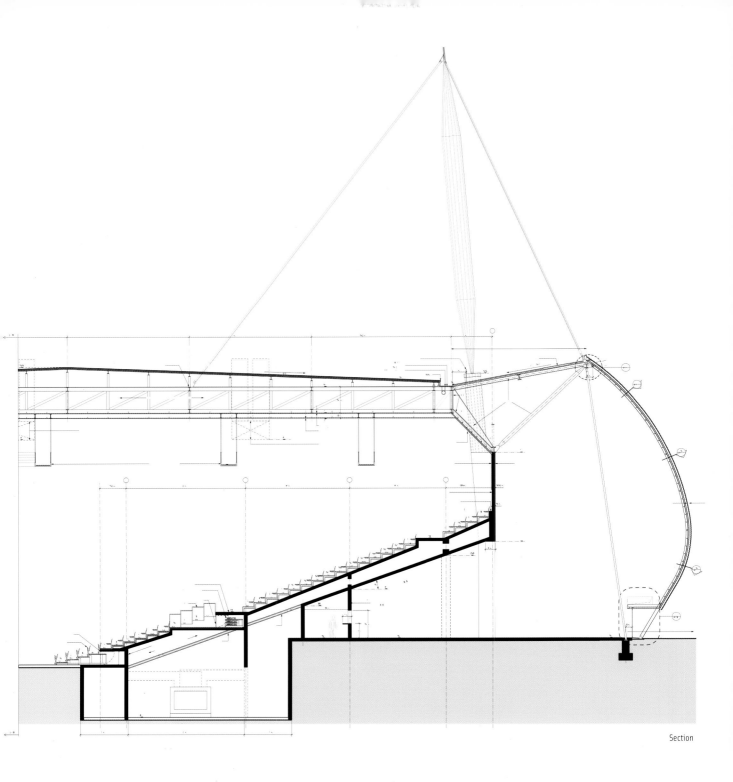

Section

Concrete construction

Precast concrete work

View (opening night)

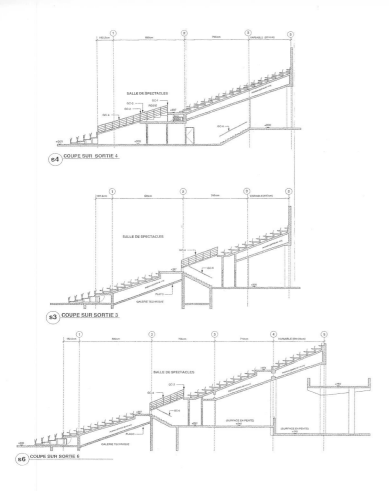

s4 COUPE SUR SORTIE 4

s3 COUPE SUR SORTIE 3

s6 COUPE SUR SORTIE 6

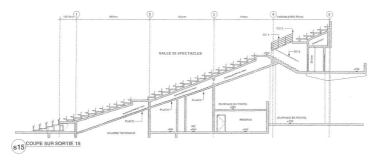

s15 COUPE SUR SORTIE 15

Sections through exits

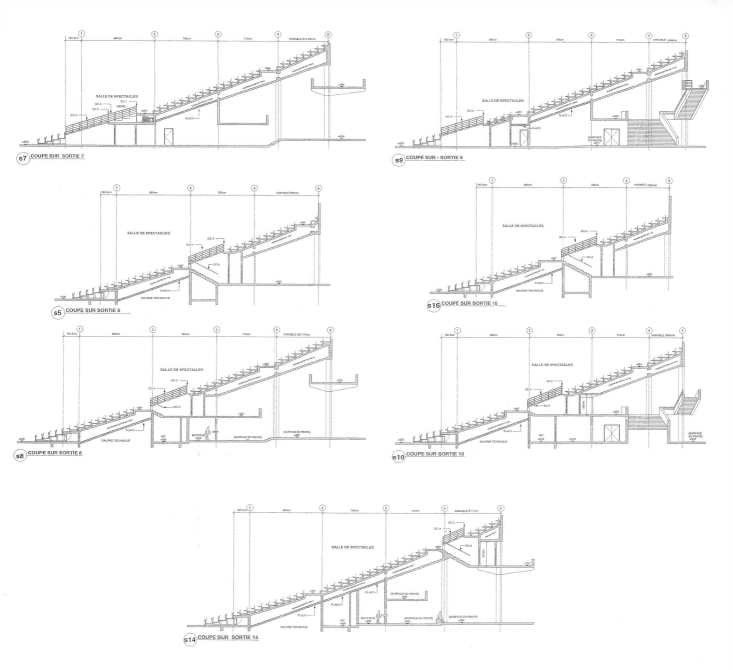

s7 COUPE SUR SORTIE 7

s9 COUPE SUR - SORTIE 9

s5 COUPE SUR SORTIE 5

s16 COUPE SUR SORTIE 16

s8 COUPE SUR SORTIE 8

s10 COUPE SUR SORTIE 10

s14 COUPE SUR SORTIE 14

Precast concrete seating construction

Stage #3

Assembly of temporary
structure to support
roof until masts and
cables were in place

Views of transition structure assembly

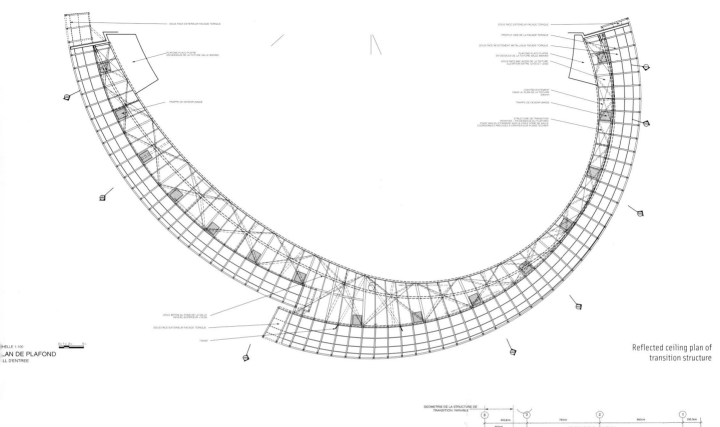

Reflected ceiling plan of
transition structure

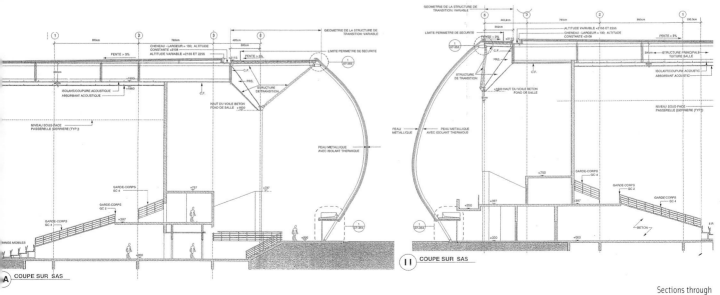

A   COUPE SUR SAS

II   COUPE SUR SAS

Sections through
transition structure

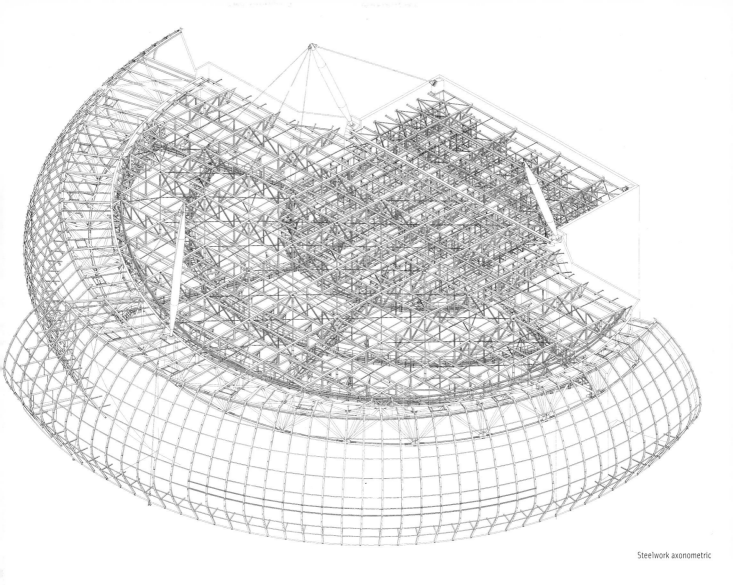

Steelwork axonometric

facing page: Assembly of roof structure

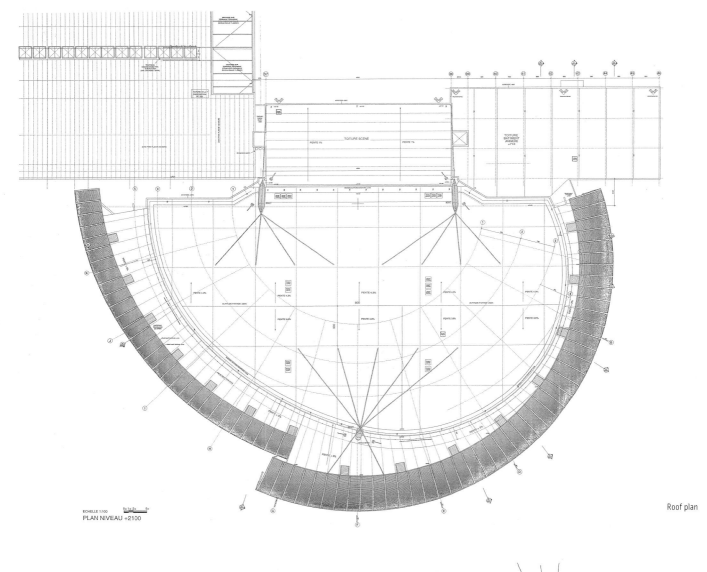

ECHELLE 1:100
PLAN NIVEAU +2100

Roof plan

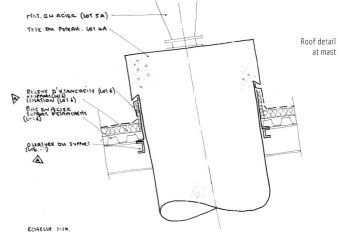

MAT. EN ACIER (LOT 5A)

TÊTE DU POTEAU. LOT 4A

RELEVÉ D'ÉTANCHÉITÉ (LOT 6)
+ SUPPORT (LOT 6)
ISOLATION (LOT 6)

BAC EN ACIER
SUPPORT D'ÉTANCHÉITÉ
(LOT 6)

OSSATURE DU SUPPORT
(LOT 6 - 1)

ECHELLE 1:10.

Roof detail
at mast

Construction photos

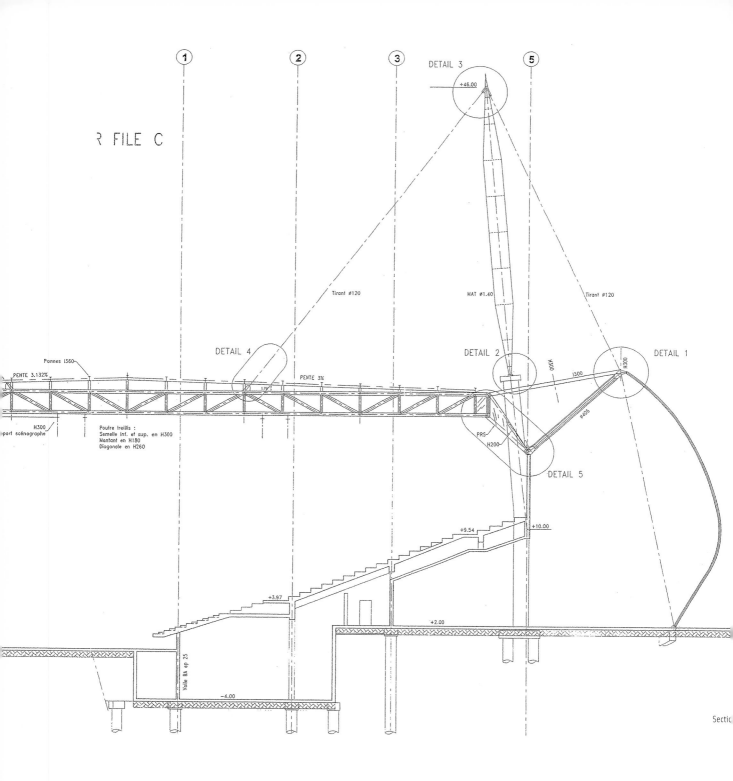

R FILE C

DETAIL 3

+46.00

Tirant ø120

MAT ø1.40

Tirant ø120

DETAIL 4

DETAIL 2

DETAIL 1

Pannes I360

PENTE 3.132%

PENTE 3%

H300

1300

H300

H300

1.79

ø406

Poutre treillis :
Semelle inf. et sup. en H300
Montant en H180
Diagonale en H260

port scénographe

PRS

H200

DETAIL 5

+9.54

+10.00

+3.97

+2.00

Voile BA ep 25

−4.00

Secti

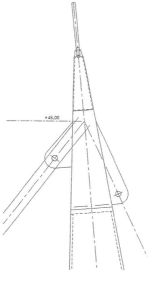

+46.00

Detail 3

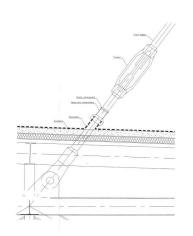

Detail 4

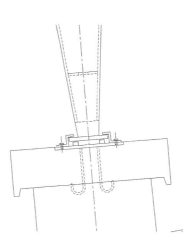

Detail 2

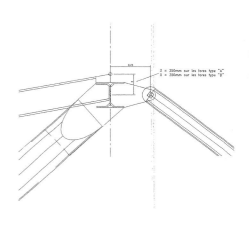

X = 250mm sur les fores type "A"
X = 350mm sur les fores type "B"

Detail 1

Mast details

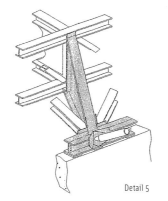

Detail 5

Interior view

Exterior view

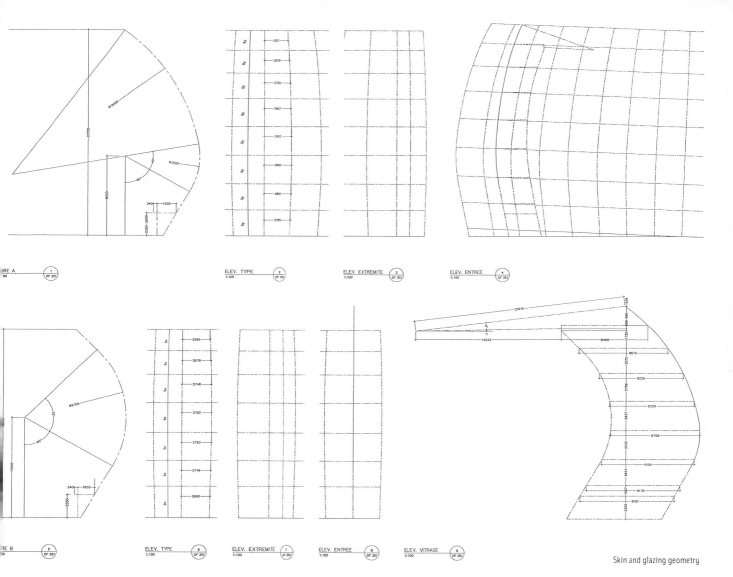

ORE A   ①   DF 351

ELEV. TYPE   1:100   ②   DF 351

ELEV. EXTREMITE   1:100   ③   DF 351

ELEV. ENTREE   1:100   ④   DF 351

RE B   ⑤   DF 351

ELEV. TYPE   1:100   ⑥   DF 351

ELEV. EXTREMITE   1:100   ⑦   DF 351

ELEV. ENTREE   1:100   ⑧   DF 351

ELEV. VITRAGE   1:100   ⑨   DF 351

Skin and glazing geometry

nsition structure, detail

Transition structure

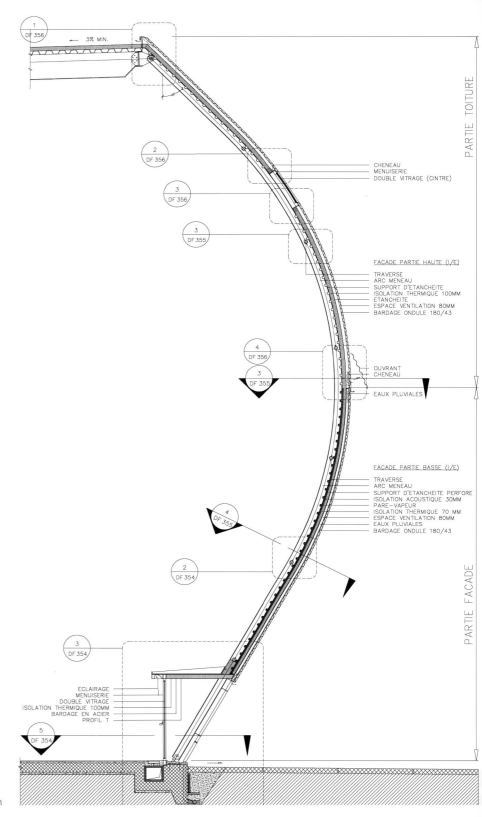

3% MIN.

1
DF 356

2
DF 356

CHENEAU
MENUISERIE
DOUBLE VITRAGE (CINTRE)

3
DF 356

3
DF 355

FACADE PARTIE HAUTE (I/E)

TRAVERSE
ARC MENEAU
SUPPORT D'ETANCHEITE
ISOLATION THERMIQUE 100MM
ETANCHEITE
ESPACE VENTILATION 80MM
BARDAGE ONDULE 180/43

4
DF 356

3
DF 355

OUVRANT
CHENEAU

EAUX PLUVIALES

FACADE PARTIE BASSE (I/E)

TRAVERSE
ARC MENEAU
SUPPORT D'ETANCHEITE PERFORE
ISOLATION ACOUSTIQUE 30MM
PARE-VAPEUR
ISOLATION THERMIQUE 70 MM
ESPACE VENTILATION 80MM
EAUX PLUVIALES
BARDAGE ONDULE 180/43

4
DF 355

2
DF 354

3
DF 354

ECLAIRAGE
MENUISERIE
DOUBLE VITRAGE
ISOLATION THERMIQUE 100MM
BARDAGE EN ACIER
PROFIL T

5
DF 354

98 EXECUTION

Section

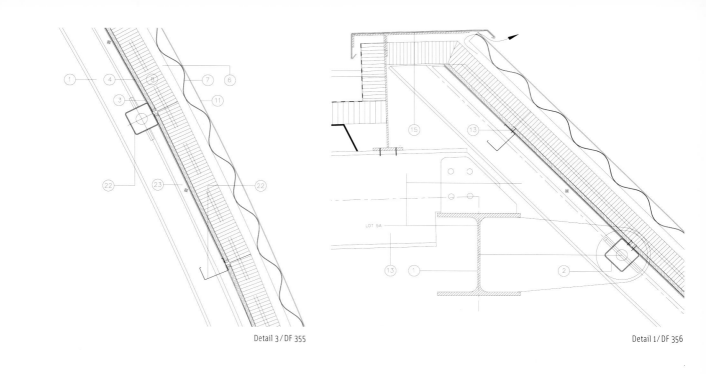

Detail 3 / DF 355

Detail 1 / DF 356

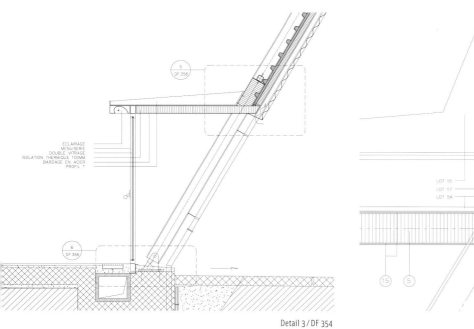

ECLAIRAGE
MENUISERIE
DOUBLE VITRAGE
ISOLATION THERMIQUE 100MM
BARDAGE EN ACIER
PROFIL T

5
DF 356

6
DF 356

Detail 3 / DF 354

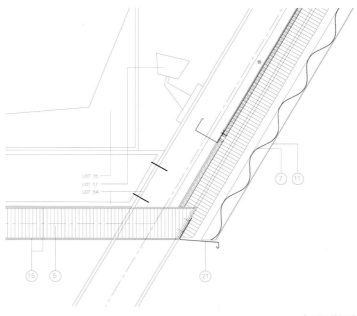

LOT 15
LOT 17
LOT 5A

Detail 5 / DF 356

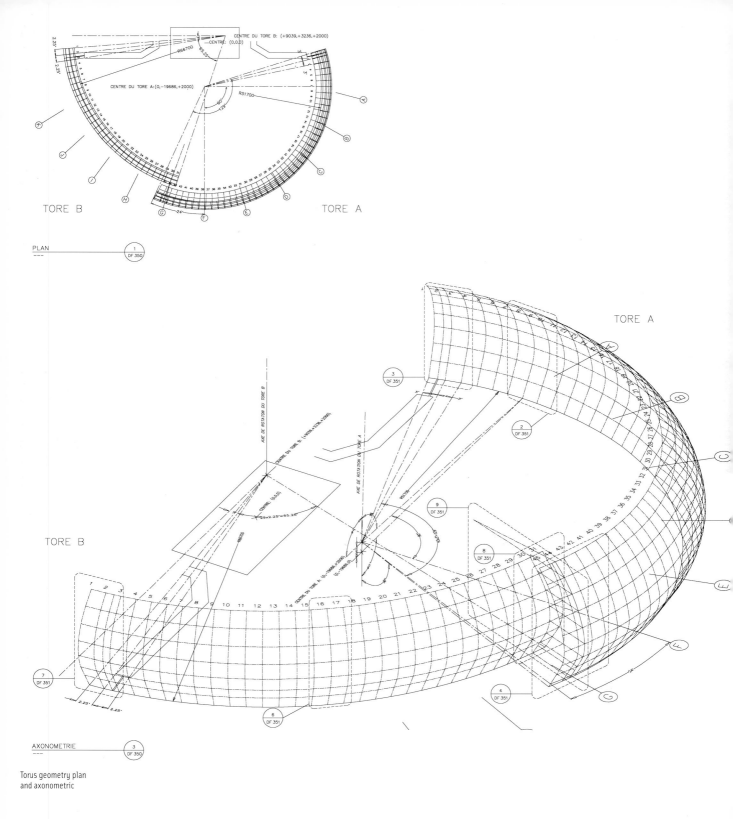

CENTRE DU TORE B: (+9039,+3236,+2000)
CENTRE: (0,0,0)
CENTRE DU TORE A: (0,−19686,+2000)
R66700
R51700

TORE B

TORE A

PLAN — 1 / DF 350

TORE A

TORE B

3 / DF 351
2 / DF 351
9 / DF 351
8 / DF 351
7 / DF 351
6 / DF 351
4 / DF 351

AXE DE ROTATION DU TORE B
CENTRE DU TORE B: (+9039,+3236,+2000)
AXE DE ROTATION DU TORE A
CENTRE: (0,0,0)
CENTRE DU TORE A: (0,−19686,+2000)

AXONOMETRIE — 3 / DF 350

Torus geometry plan
and axonometric

View

Assembly views of
torus structure

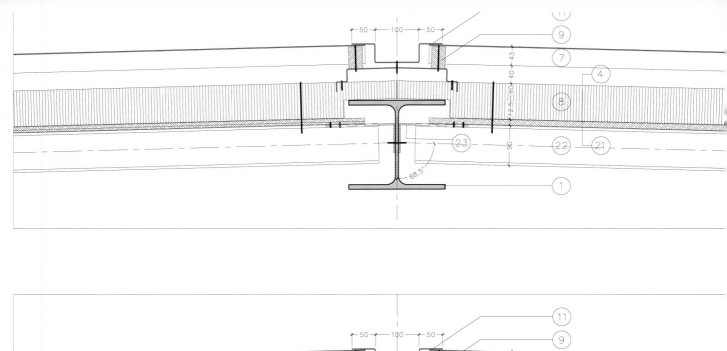

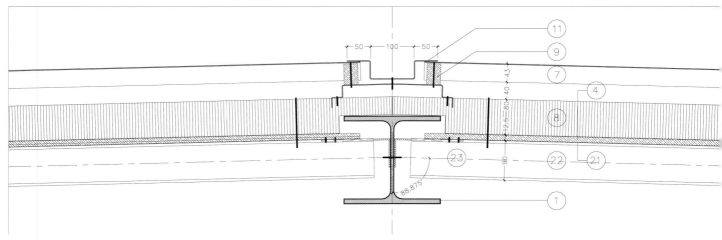

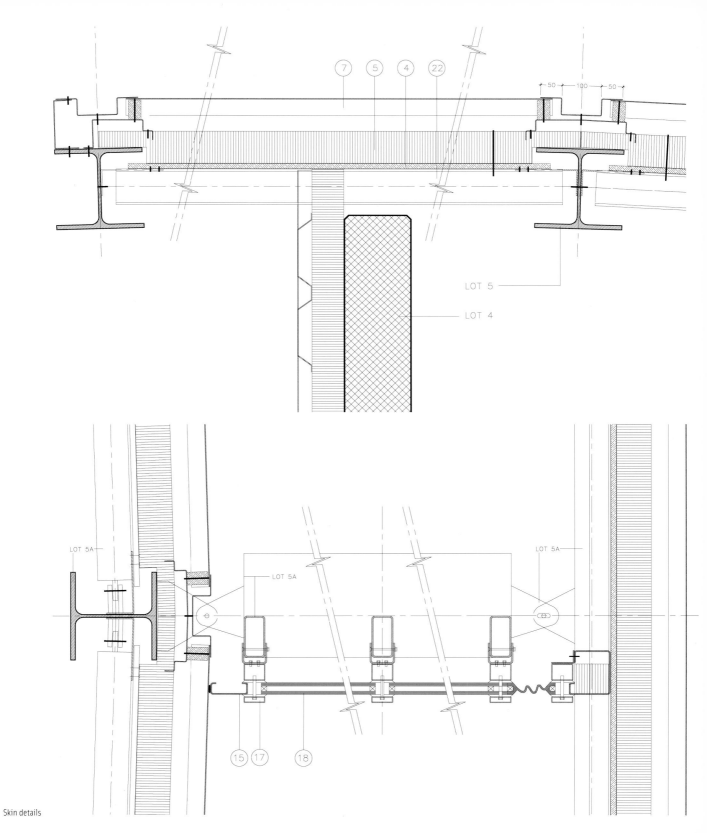

Skin details

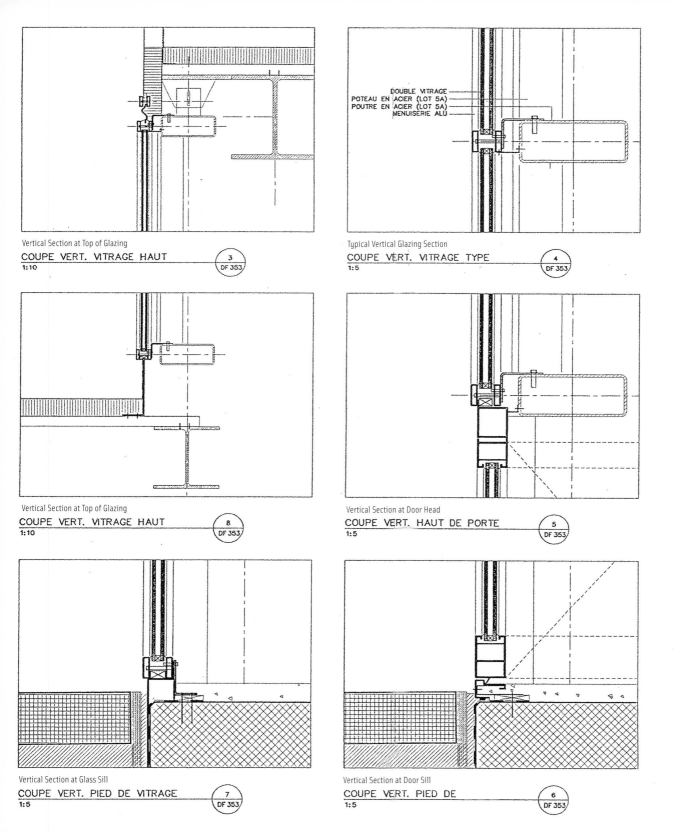

Vertical Section at Top of Glazing
COUPE VERT. VITRAGE HAUT
1:10

3
DF 353

Typical Vertical Glazing Section
COUPE VERT. VITRAGE TYPE
1:5

4
DF 353

DOUBLE VITRAGE
POTEAU EN ACIER (LOT 5A)
POUTRE EN ACIER (LOT 5A)
MENUISERIE ALU

Vertical Section at Top of Glazing
COUPE VERT. VITRAGE HAUT
1:10

8
DF 353

Vertical Section at Door Head
COUPE VERT. HAUT DE PORTE
1:5

5
DF 353

Vertical Section at Glass Sill
COUPE VERT. PIED DE VITRAGE
1:5

7
DF 353

Vertical Section at Door Sill
COUPE VERT. PIED DE
1:5

6
DF 353

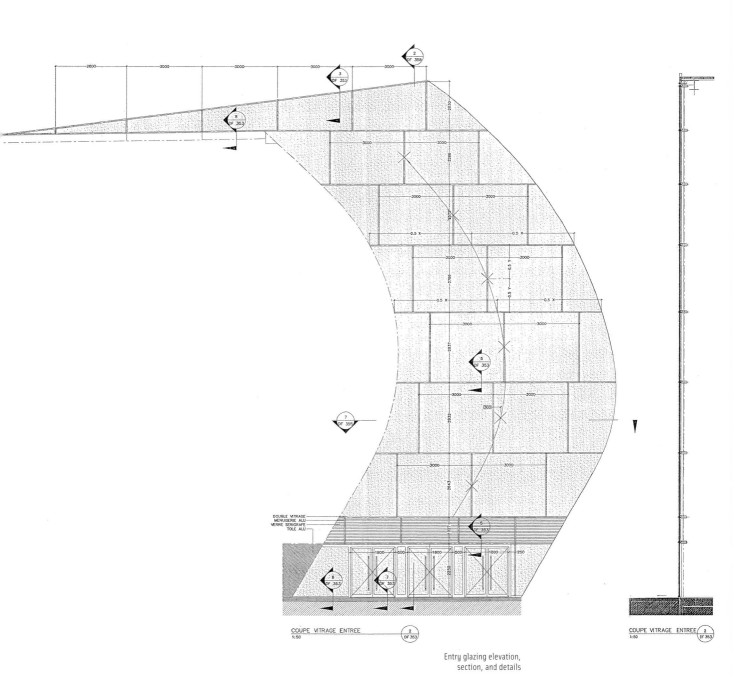

COUPE VITRAGE ENTREE (2 DF 353)
1:50

COUPE VITRAGE ENTREE (2 DF 353)
1:50

Entry glazing elevation,
section, and details

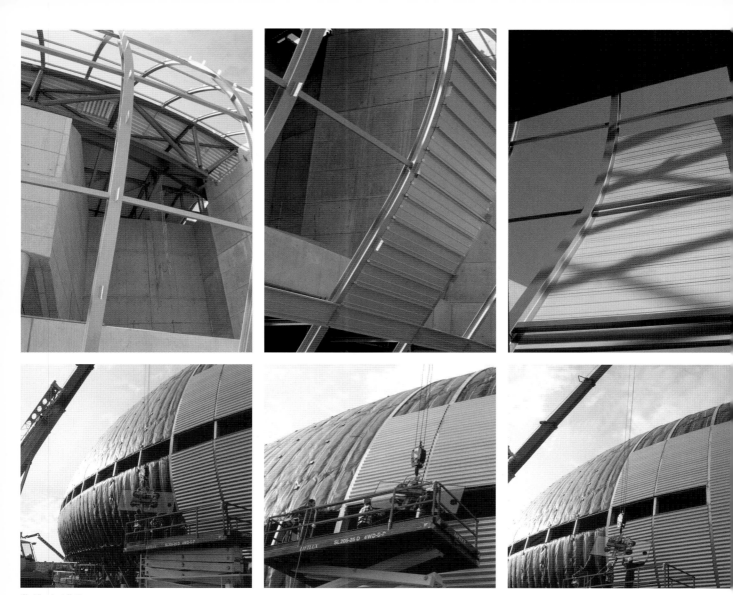

Cladding installation

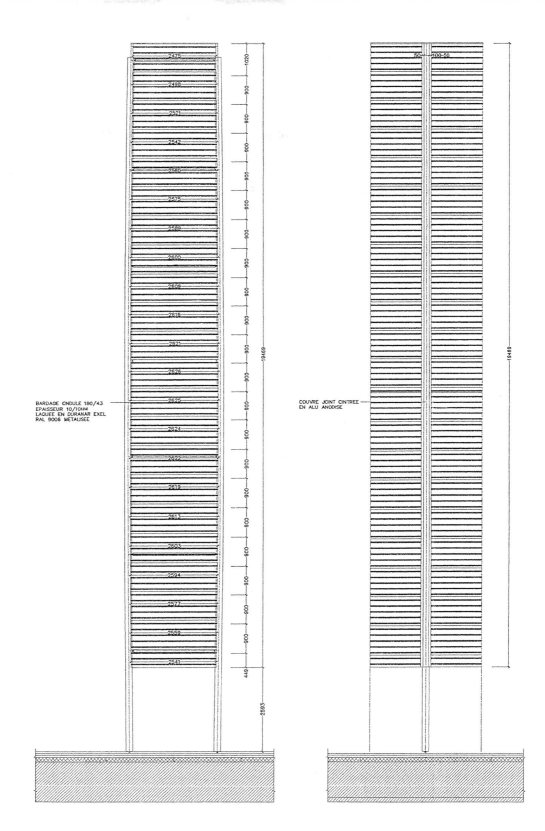

BARDAGE ONDULE 180/43
EPAISSEUR 10/10MM
LAQUEE EN DURANAR EXEL
RAL 9006 METALISEE

COUVRE JOINT CINTREE
EN ALU ANODISE

Elevation details, skin

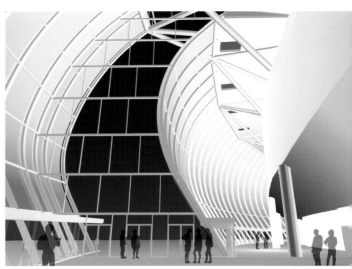
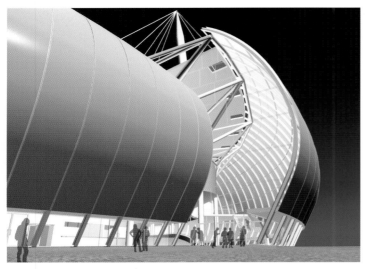

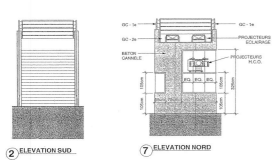

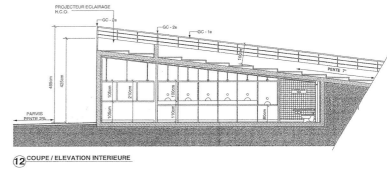

(2) ELEVATION SUD

South Elevation

(7) ELEVATION NORD

North Elevation

(12) COUPE / ELEVATION INTERIEURE

Section/Interior Elevation

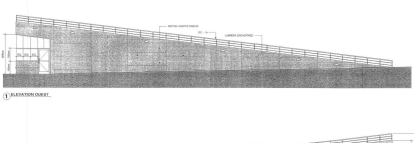

(1) ELEVATION OUEST

East Elevation

(6) ELEVATION EST

Section/Interior Elevation

(11) COUPE / ELEVATION INTERIEURE

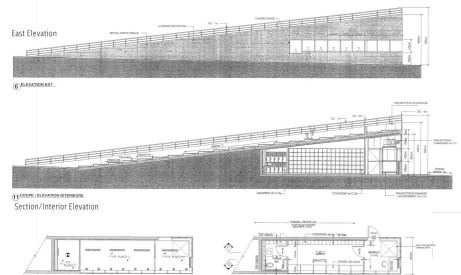

(13) PLAN DE PLAFOND

(14) PLAN

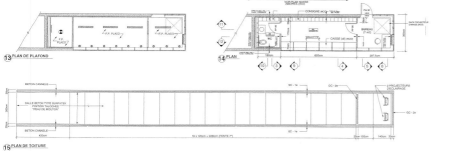

(15) PLAN DE TOITURE

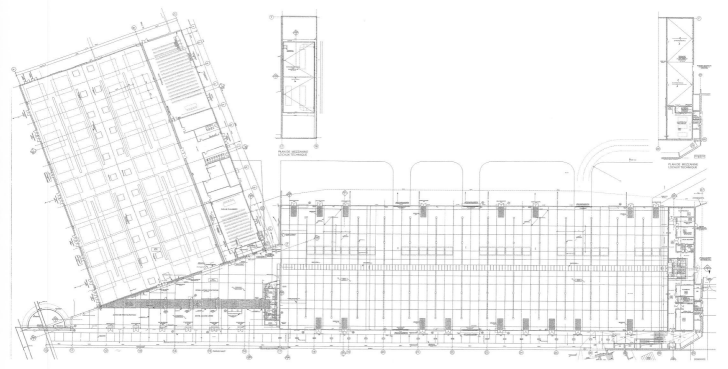

Exhibition Hall plan

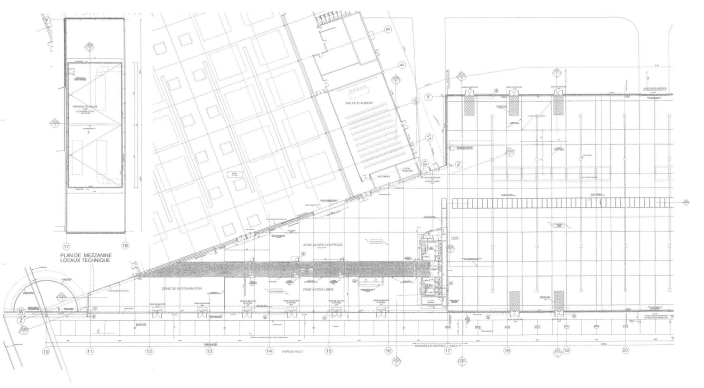

Exhibition Hall entry plan

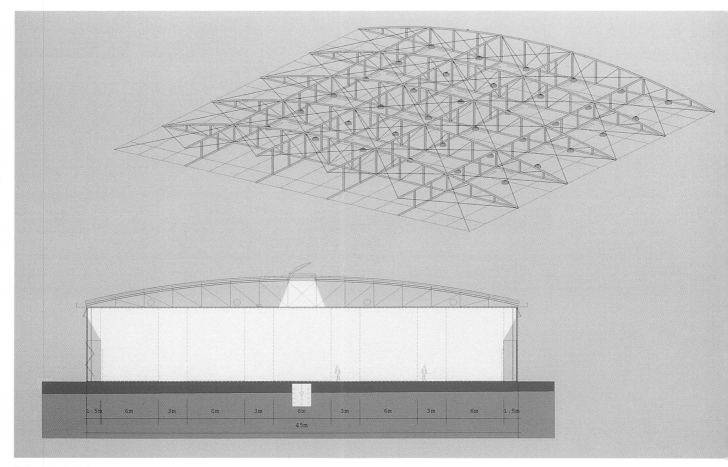

1.5m | 6m | 3m | 6m | 3m | 6m | 3m | 6m | 3m | 6m | 1.5m

45m

Section and roof structure
axonometric

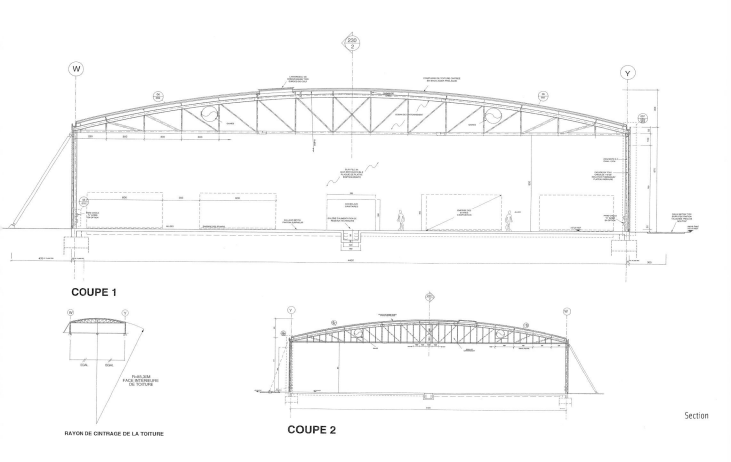

COUPE 1

RAYON DE CINTRAGE DE LA TOITURE

R=85,30M
FACE INTERIEURE
DE TOITURE

EGAL   EGAL

COUPE 2

Section

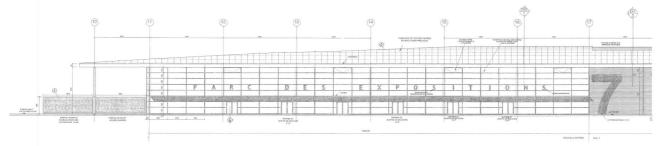

Exhibition Hall entry elevation

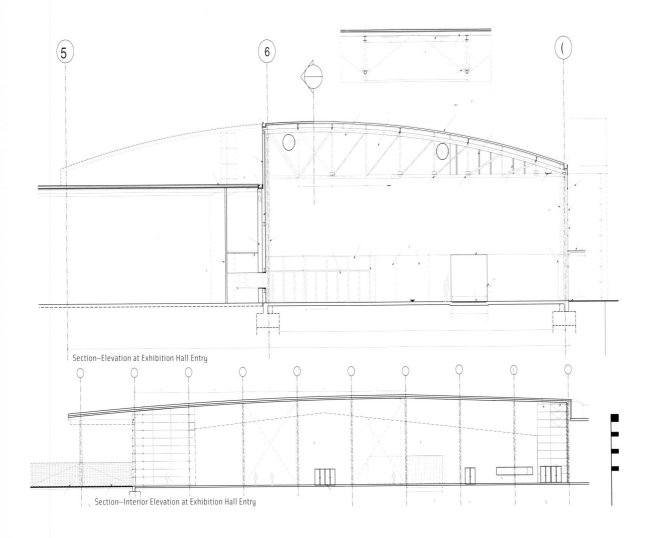

Section–Elevation at Exhibition Hall Entry

Section–Interior Elevation at Exhibition Hall Entry

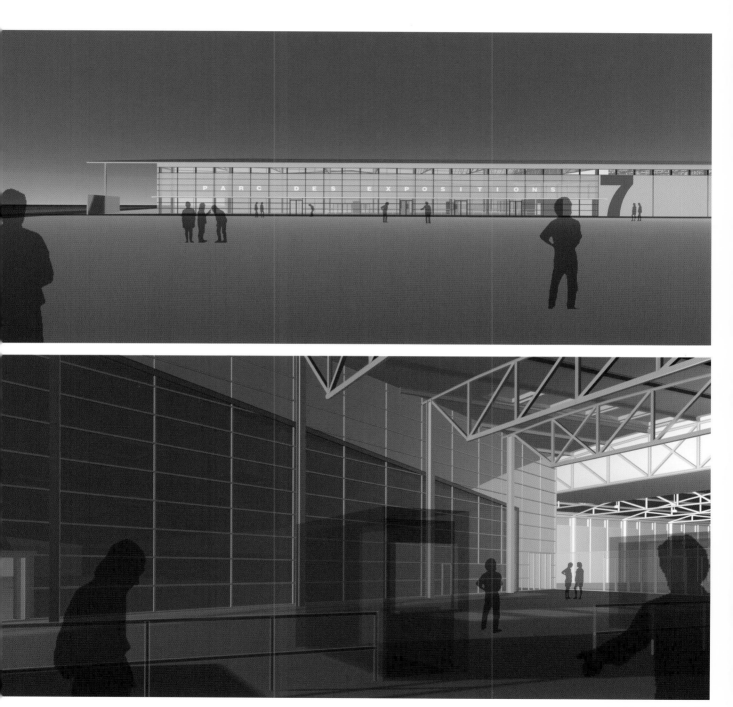

top: Entrance to Exhibition Hall

above: Interior perspective

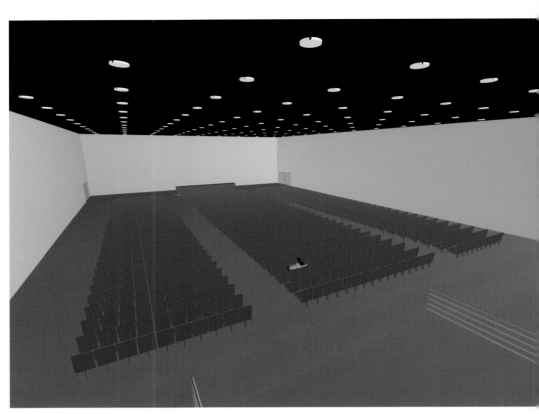

Hall 9
Interior View

Hall 7
Interior view

top and left: Hall 7
during construction

Exhibition Hall
glazing construction

Construction photos

West facade of Hall 7 with
exterior lateral bracing

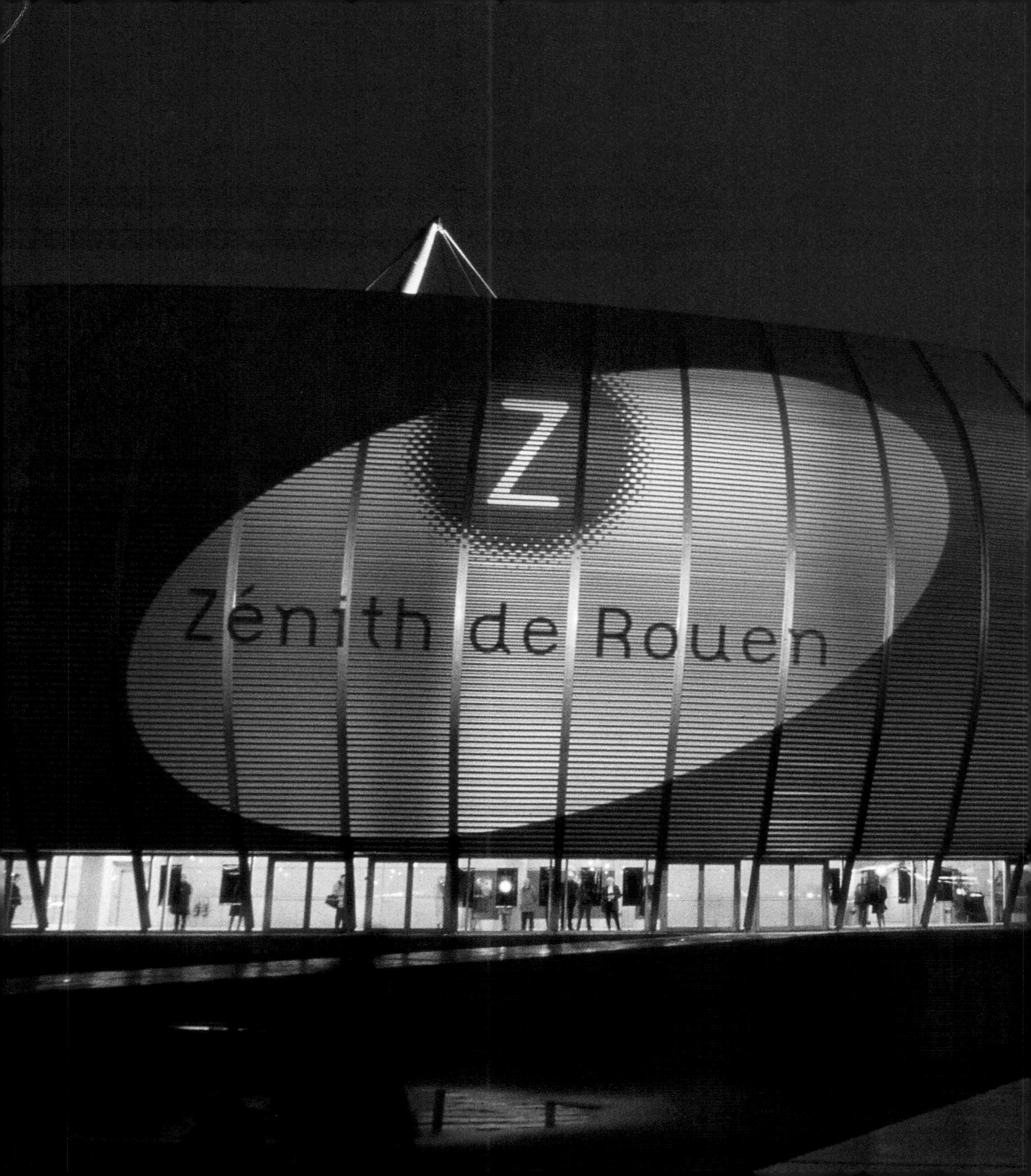
Z
Zénith de Rouen

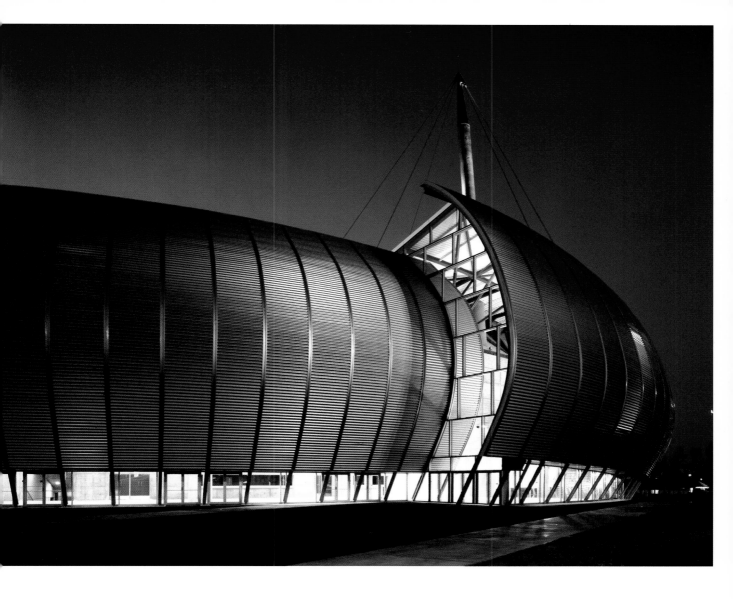

TSCHUMI'S ROADSIDE ATTRACTION
Todd Gannon

Big, undifferentiated buildings, built cheap and fast and surrounded by a sea of asphalt, are the stuff of the contemporary roadside. Regardless of whether they reside outside Indianapolis or Athens, they all look pretty much the same. Long ago we quit noticing this ubiquitous landscape of big boxes, parking lots, telephone poles and power lines, preferring a single blurred continuum as we hurtle past at seventy miles per hour. But every once in a while, a defiant building refuses to fade quietly into the banal milieu. Through accident or intention, these renegade few demand closer scrutiny. On an unassuming stretch of highway a few miles south of Rouen, France, lies one such building: Bernard Tschumi's Zénith Concert Hall.

A cursory survey of massing and materials reveals nothing out of the ordinary: it is big (over 1000 feet long), blank, and for the most part unarticulated. It boasts precious few windows, off-the-shelf garage doors, and it is clad in the same corrugated metal of countless suburban warehouses. In keeping with the roadside standard, acres of asphalt and the obligatory strip of lawn provide a buffer from the traffic speeding past.

Affinities of scale and material are reaffirmed by the site plan, which discloses an unpretentious collection of warehouse buildings, two aligning with adjacent roads, the others loosely defining a central courtyard. It all seems perfectly ordinary, except for the bulbous

protrusion from the easternmost shed. Describing an aggressive curve in plan and section, its metal skin bulges precariously toward the roadway, as if the shed were gestating something terrible. Tall masts and steel cables seem to keep everything at bay, but a threatening gash of ribbon window suggests that it will not hold together for long.

Driving past, this strange object appears to rotate, as if pivoting about one of its rooftop spires. Turning back to gape after passing from the north reveals another surprise. This balloonlike volume is not a volume at all, but rather two thin planes, pinned at the ground and lashed at the top, their middles thrust forward by some unseen force.

What are we to make of this unearthly roadside attraction? At first pass, a critic might be tempted to associate the conspicuous steel masts, stay cables, and billowing facades with the maritime history of Rouen. From there it would be an easy leap from the tectonics of sailing vessels to an analysis of frames clad in fabric à la Gottfried Semper. A grimmer reading might suggest that the curved, feminine forms bound to vertical stakes recall the martyrdom of Joan of Arc, Rouen's patron saint. If not careful, a well-meaning critic might find himself spinning fantastical yarns that place Tschumi's concert hall in the unlikely company of religious monuments and the primitive hut!

But perhaps this Semperian observation may reveal some insight. The building does call to mind a frame-and-fabric structure, though not necessarily Semper's primal wellspring of architectural form. Rather, the Rouen Concert Hall evokes a different building type, less venerated but more aligned with Tschumi's predilection for the spectacle. Reviving an abandoned site on the outskirts of town, the concert hall is not so much sacred temple as circus tent.

Architecture, the historians tell us, is about permanence and stability. Think pyramids, temples, and cathedrals—widely disparate archetypes that nonetheless share a privileged position in the canon and a reliance on the durability of masonry construction. The circus tent derives from a different lineage—one equally distinguished yet less concerned with leaving behind the evidence. From Bedouin oasis to Boy Scout camp, temporary structures throughout history engage us with all the intensity of their more lasting counterparts. If the most permanent buildings are masonry and therefore compressive, then the most ephemeral are surely tensile.

Tensile structures, like Tschumi himself, deal not with forms but with events. Their visceral tension derives not from material properties but from a latent impermanence. An affront to gravity itself, a structure in tension suspends more than physical mass; it suspends the certainty of its eventual collapse.

Thrown up overnight, the circus tent is one of these tensile wonders. Its enormous scale and bright colors mark the landscape as dramatically as any masonry pile of architectural history, but this monument does not last. As magically as it appeared, the whole thing is packed up, again under cover of night, and vanishes. The Rouen Concert Hall, while decidedly more permanent, makes this fleeting imagery its own. The masts and stay cables appear to be pulling the curved walls into position, as if we had inadvertently happened upon one of these clandestine nocturnal constructions. Or perhaps we are witnessing the reverse—a veil or curtain being cast off to reveal the spectacle within.

And when we consider the kinds of spectacles that grace the Rouen Concert Hall, we find even more affinities with the renegade tactics of Bernard Tschumi. For while most concert halls of architectural import defer to the needs of classical music, Rouen, with its amplified interior and absorptive acoustics, was made to rock.

Both Tschumi and rock music were born circa 1950 and matured in the political and social turmoil of the late sixties. Both share with their cousin the circus a taste for the spectacular, and all rely on precision, roughness, and shock in equal measure. Tschumi is at his best when working along these lines, which perhaps accounts for his uncomfortable intervention at Columbia University. Genuflecting to McKim, Mead and White's austere beaux arts campus, Lerner Hall resembles a mischievous child dressed up for the holidays, the irritation with its surroundings clear and its true impudence suppressed to the interior.

At Rouen, Tschumi revels in this youthful energy. The building is stripped down; like rock music it prefers to do a lot with a little. The restrained pallette of materials– concrete, steel, and glass—recalls the power trio, rock's tried-and-true formula of drums, bass, and guitar. Interior concrete columns march in loose syncopation with the curved steel structure of the exterior skin, while stairs and ramps crescendo dramatically between. The asymmetrical arrangement denies the centripetal focus of typical theaters and instead draws our eye to the directional flow of the periphery, where the three materials trade solos, weaving in and out of the spotlight of our attention. As such, the building pays homage to the great halls of Jørn Utzon and Hans Scharoun, though here Tschumi distills the symphonic richness of Sydney and Berlin to deliver a more forceful wallop.

To achieve this no-frills effect in a building of this scale requires a particular diligence of the architect. The demands of mechanical distribution, fireproofing, lateral bracing and other tectonic considerations, the interior corollaries of the roadside junk mentioned earlier, all conspire to muddy such clarity of intention. Other architects might celebrate this cacophony of architectural tackle, but Tschumi suppresses it, staying true to the frankness of rock and roll. Double-walled seating construction conceals air distribution save for a single friezelike duct that runs the length of the concourse. Light fixtures hide behind this ring of metal like roadies lurking backstage. Diagonal bracing was mini-

mized, and an excessive number of exits were employed to allow the omission of interior fireproofing, maintaining the crispness of the steel structure. The effect is at once unabashedly visceral and highly abstract, the vastness of the space made palpable by its spare definition. During performances, dramatic lighting and frenetic crowds increase its efficacy, dematerializing the structure to near pure sensation.

By employing such stringent techniques, Tschumi avoids the pitfalls that subtly undermine the strength of his previous work. At Rouen, off-the-shelf components do not distract our attention, as the fetishized details do at Columbia and even at Le Fresnoy. Inside, space and movement take center stage, making the work a tour de force of unbridled affect and Tschumi's most convincing rendition of Event Space to date.

PROJECT CREDITS

CLIENT
District of Rouen, France

ARCHITECT
Bernard Tschumi Architects
Bernard Tschumi, principal

PARIS OFFICE
Véronique Descharrières
Alex Reid
Cristina Devizzi
Laurane Ponsonnet

NEW YORK OFFICE
Kevin Collins
Peter Cornell
Robert Holton
Megan Miller
Joel Rutten
Kim Starr
Roderick Villafranca

CONSULTANTS
ENVELOPE AND FACADE
Hugh Dutton (HDA), Paris

STRUCTURAL ENGINEERING
Technip-TPS

MECHANICAL ENGINEERING
Technip Seri

ACOUSTICS
Cabinet Cial

THEATER CONSULTANT
Deuxième Acte

GENERAL CONTRACTOR
Quille

GENERAL SPECIFICATIONS
STRUCTURAL SYSTEM
SMB (metal)
Quille (concrete)

EXTERIOR CLADDING
Quille
(masonry and concrete)
SMB and Julien
(metal/glass curtain wall)

ROOFING
Spada (Built-up roofing)
Etanchisa (metal)

WINDOWS
Rineau (steel)
Pilkinton; St Gobain (glass)

DOORS
Metallerie Houlnoise (metal)

HARDWARE
Cerberus (security device)

INTERIOR FINISHES
Acoustisol + Plaquistes Pecards
(acoustical ceiling)
Scenetec (suspension grid)

FIXED SEATING
Grofilex (Siege BTA-modèle
Dépose)

LIGHTING
Szen-S3en (interior ambient)

CONVEYING SYSTEMS
Thyssen

PLUMBING
Porraz

PHOTOGRAPHY
All photos provided by Bernard
Tschumi Architects except
as follows:

Peter Mauss/ESTO, pp. 140-141,
143, 144, 145, 148, 150, 151 bottom
left and right, 152, 153, 154

Robert Cesar, pp. 142, 149,
151 top

Todd Gannon, pp. 121 top,
middle, and bottom right

Bernard Tschumi Architects. "Performance Hall and Exhibition Centre, Rouen, France." *Architectural Design* 69, no. 3/4 (March/April 1999): 62–65.

Florence, Michel. "Tschumi a Rouen" (Tschumi in Rouen). *Domus* 838 (June 2001): 56–67.

Melvin, Jeremy. "So Tschumi." *RIBA Journal* 108, no. 5 (May 2001): 10–11.

Raymund, Ryan. "Rouen's Zénith: Conference Center and Concert Hall, Rouen, France." *Architectural Review* 210, no. 1254 (August 2001): 55–59.

Stephens, Suzanne. "Zénith Concert Hall, Rouen, France." *Architectural Record* 189, no. 6 (June 2001): 102–11.

Tschumi, Bernard. "Concert Hall and Exhibition Complex (Zénith), Rouen, France." *GA Document* 67 (October 2001): 760–83.

———. *Event-Cities* (Cambridge: MIT Press, 1999).

———. *Event-Cities 2.* (Cambridge: MIT Press, 2000).

———. *The Manhattan Transcripts* (London: Academy Editions; New York: St. Martin's Press, 1994).

———. "Rouen Concert Hall and Exhibition Complex, Rouen, France." *GA Document* 58 (April 1999): 96–99.

———. *Tschumi Le Fresnoy: Architecture In/Between* (New York: Monacelli Press, 1999).

Yoshida, Nobuyuki. "Performance Hall and Exhibition Center in Rouen, France 1998–2000." *A + U: Architecture and Urbanism* 334, no. 7 (July 1998): 12–23.

BIOGRAPHIES

Todd Gannon is a lecturer in architectural theory and design at the Knowlton School of Architecture and a project designer at Acock Associates Architects in Columbus, Ohio. Previous books include *Morphosis/Diamond Ranch High School* and *The Light Construction Reader*.

Jeffrey Kipnis, professor of architecture at the Knowlton School of Architecture was formerly curator of architecture at the Wexner Center for the Arts and director of the graduate design program at the Architectural Association in London. He has taught and lectured at schools of architecture worldwide and is a frequent contributor to architectural magazines and journals. Recent works include *Mood River*, *Perfect Acts of Architecture*, and the documentary film *A Constructive Madness*.

Laurie Gunzelman is a graduate of the Knowlton School of Architecture and a designer with Jonathan Barnes Architecture and Design, in Columbus, Ohio.